simple crochet

simple crochet

ERIKA KNIGHT

photographs by
John Heseltine

CLARKSON POTTER/PUBLISHERS
NEW YORK

Copyright © 2003 Quadrille Publishing Limited
Text copyright © 2003 Erika Knight

All rights reserved. No part of this book may be reproduced or transmitted in any form or by any means, electronic or mechanical, including photocopying, recording, or by any information storage and retrieval system, without permission in writing from the publisher.

Published by Clarkson Potter/Publishers, New York, New York. Member of the Crown Publishing Group, a division of Random House, Inc.
www.crownpublishing.com

CLARKSON N. POTTER is a trademark and POTTER and colophon are registered trademarks of Random House, Inc.

Printed in China

Created by Susan Berry and Erika Knight
Project Director, Susan Berry
Designer, Anne Wilson
Editor, Sally Harding
Stylist, Julia Bird

Library of Congress Cataloging-in-Publication Data is available on request.

ISBN 1-4000-5079-0
10 9 8 7 6 5 4
First Edition

contents

introduction

As we begin to reassess our lifestyles, we will find inspiration at home and in traditional values. Cherishing the personal and the hand-made is part of this, as we seek to surround ourselves with things that are precious to us. Hand-made textiles offer a unique opportunity to express our creativity in simple yet enduring ways, and there is no easier form of this than crochet. Basic yet intricate, delicate yet robust, practical yet decorative, it creates a fabric that has a beautiful and interesting texture. Moreover, as I hope this book demonstrates, it is also amazingly versatile.

"I believe in making things simple and in making simple things."

Crochet is much easier than knitting, using only one hook and a ball of yarn, and it is easy to carry around, so you can do it anywhere—on the train, the bus, the plane, in your lunch break, or while waiting for your children in the playground. With only a little practice you will find your fingers working to a rhythm. You can crochet while you chat to friends or listen to the radio or to music, so you make the best use of your increasingly precious time. It is, undoubtedly, a form of yoga for the hands.

Simple Crochet is what it says. It concentrates on a few basic stitches, and some very different types of yarn. With just this, you are able to make almost anything. Moreover, crochet is quick; most of the projects in this book take only a few evenings at most. So, with luck, you will actually finish a project! Too many of us have embarked on crafts we have found complicated, and the half-finished remnants still lurk in the back of our dressers and closets.

"You can create a fabric with crochet from almost any length of continuous fiber."

String, rags, and leather—you name it, you can crochet with it. The materials are easy to locate: you can even find them in the garden shed or the hardware store as well as in the local yarn shop. Experimenting is the key. Feel the different textures, the natural touch, and have fun with nontraditional materials, too. The fabric that crochet makes is firm and textural, but endlessly versatile. The projects I have chosen for this book, I hope, make crochet modern and interesting. Use crochet imaginatively to create textiles that offer a visual surprise: mix delicate items with modern, hard-edged surfaces or combine tough string pillows with delicate antique linen, for example.

But most important of all, in making crochet, you create something that is very much your own—personal, beautiful, and long lasting.

Release your creativity!

Erika Knight

yarns

1

2

5

6

9

10

8

You can crochet with a wonderful range of yarns, to produce some excitingly varied textiles. The yarn and stitch chosen will determine the character of the crochet. Examples are shown on pages 10–11.

below Just some of the yarns at your disposal, including soft cotton (**1**), hemp (**2**), metallic thread (**3**), heavy-weight string (**4**), ribbon (**5**), leather (**6**), linen (**7**), thick cotton (**8**), dyed cotton (**9**), natural cotton (**10**), fine cotton (**11**), and mohair (**12**).

3

4

7

8

11

12

texture

Crochet is one of the most basic forms of textile, having at its roots an affinity with fisherman's nets and medieval lace. The inspiration for this book is the very different materials with which you can crochet using only the most basic, easy-to-work stitches. Crochet can be worked in rows or in the round, and squares or strips of crochet can be joined together to make patchworks or throws.

You can use the texture of crochet in many ways, sometimes with dramatic results. Some projects in this book have been made from unusual materials: leather, raffia, or string. Some have a tight, dense, and firm structure, while others are more open and flexible. For the latter, yarns such as metallic thread or mercerized cotton are ideal. Woven effects can be created for functional rugs and throws—using old fabrics cut into strips works brilliantly for this kind of texture. To emphasize the versatility of crochet, you can even create sculptural items using tough yarns such as sisal or hemp.

The choice of yarn and fabric will be determined by the form and function of the textile. A floor pillow requires a heavy-duty, robust thread that will stand plenty of wear and tear. Leather is a great choice as its appearance improves with wear, but it is not the cheapest of materials. Sisal and hemp are less expensive and look good, too, as do strips of fabric cut from old denim jeans and jackets, for example, both tough enough for hard-wearing longevity.

The samples, right, show you the variations in texture and form that can be achieved using a variety of different threads and yarns.

Soft cotton is light and warm. It is ideal for soft, flexible fabrics for pillows or throws.

Leather has a brilliant sheen and is very durable. Use it for stylish interiors, in the form of containers or floor pillows.

Ribbon makes a soft, elegant, feminine-looking fabric that is cool and lightweight. Use it for pillows or throws.

Thick cotton is soft, smooth and very warm. It has great stitch clarity. Use it for blankets and throws.

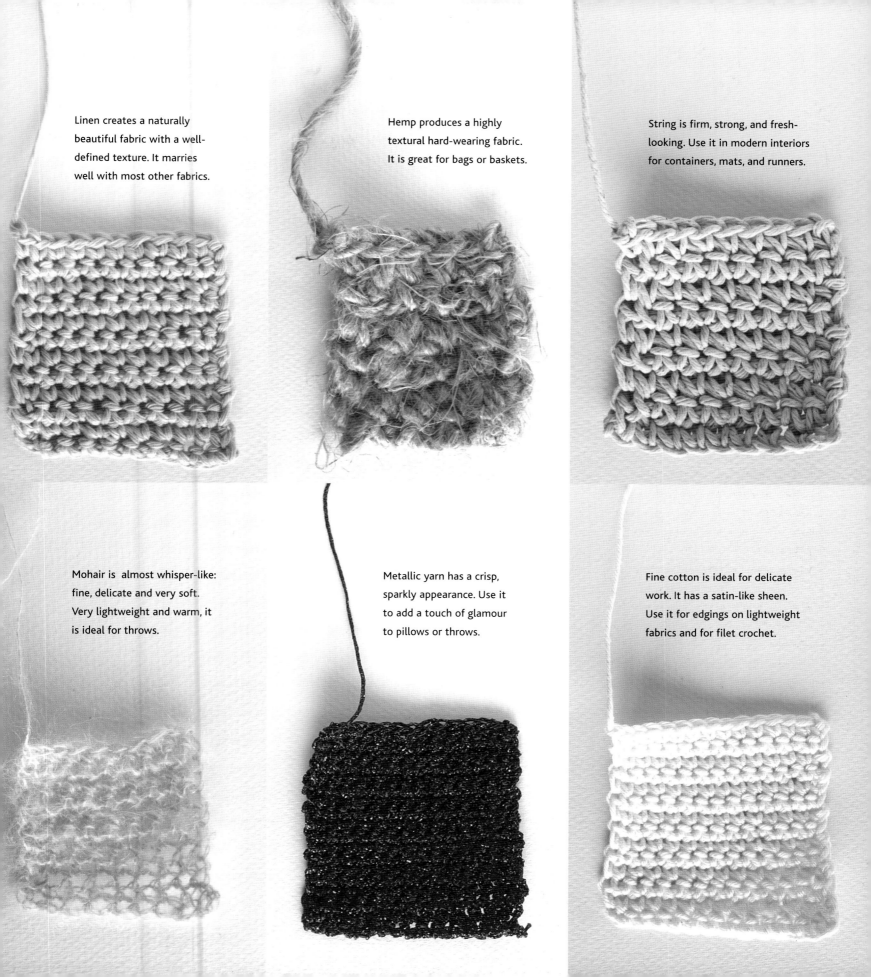

Linen creates a naturally beautiful fabric with a well-defined texture. It marries well with most other fabrics.

Hemp produces a highly textural hard-wearing fabric. It is great for bags or baskets.

String is firm, strong, and fresh-looking. Use it in modern interiors for containers, mats, and runners.

Mohair is almost whisper-like: fine, delicate and very soft. Very lightweight and warm, it is ideal for throws.

Metallic yarn has a crisp, sparkly appearance. Use it to add a touch of glamour to pillows or throws.

Fine cotton is ideal for delicate work. It has a satin-like sheen. Use it for edgings on lightweight fabrics and for filet crochet.

color

Choosing appropriate colors is both exciting and challenging. My own color palette tends toward natural colors and monochromes as a base, with touches of brighter color to give it life and luster. I find that this works well in most interior schemes, and provides a bridge between contemporary style and the much-loved pieces of furniture that all of us gather as our lives progress.

NATURAL COLORS

In the natural color palette, undyed yarns, simple kitchen twine, and cool monochromes work well with modern interiors—light woods, glass, leather, brick, plaster, and metal. If you have a minimalist interior, this palette will complement it, but the textiles will add a necessary touch of softness and luxury. Texture adds sparkle to a surface, particularly when you use contrasts: matte with shiny, thick with thin, and soft with hard. Combine metallic yarns with leather, for example, or use soft linen on bleached wood or glass.

COLOR WITH NATURAL

In the color-with-natural palette, you can add small touches of color to neutrals to provide "hot spots" in an otherwise simple scheme. Add a bright border to a plain throw or container, add stripes of strong reds or pinks to a runner with a neutral ground, or add toning borders or stripes in soft greens and browns.

COLOR ON COLOR

To create vibrancy, my personal passion is for pinks and greens in every hue, which work with the natural palette and also give a traditional look a modern twist, especially when spiced with a dash of orange or mango, or with just a hint of pomegranate. Clash colors, and keep the surprises coming!

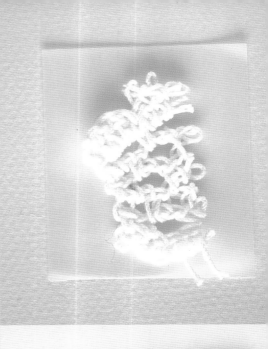
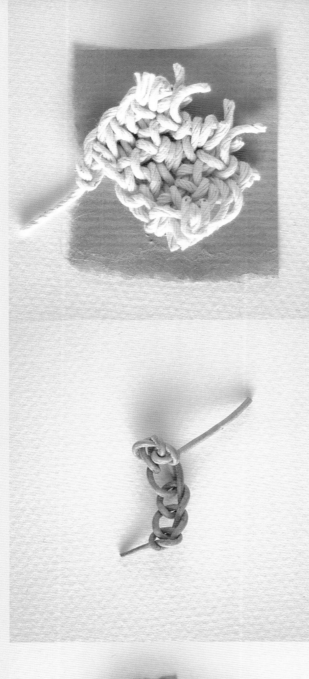

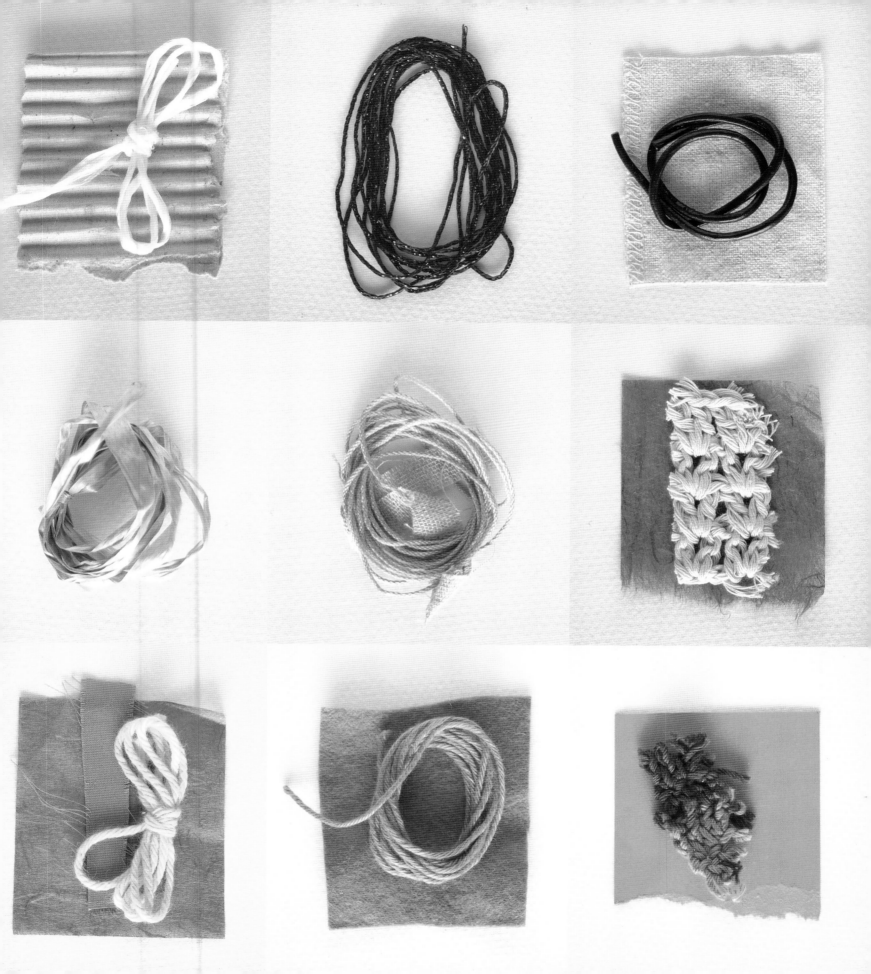

crochet basics

equipment & gauge

You really need very little equipment for crochet. The most important item is the crochet hook. I like to work with bamboo hooks, because not only are they made from a natural material, they have a very smooth finish, so that the yarn slides easily over the tip.

It is important when crocheting to feel comfortable with the way you hold the hook and yarn, and you should practice the basic techniques shown on pages 18–27 until you are comfortable with the process.

The hooks come in various sizes, from very fine (size 14 steel/ .60mm) to very thick (size Q/16.00mm). Those shown right are the most commonly used sizes in this book. Fine threads will usually require a fine hook, while chunky cottons or string need the larger sizes. (For hook conversion chart, see page 121.)

In addition to your hooks, you will need a large-eyed sewing needle with a blunt tip (a "yarn" or "tapestry" needle) and a pair of sharp dressmakers' scissors. A tape measure or ruler is useful, too.

stitch size (gauge)

Everyone who makes textiles works with a different tension. Your "tension" is how tightly or loosely you make the crochet loops (your stitch size). This means that the size of the stitch (called the gauge) will vary from crocheter to crocheter, even when the same yarn and hook size is used. Crochet patterns are designed with a specific stitch size in mind, so it is best to test your stitch size before starting your crochet project—otherwise it may turn out bigger or smaller than planned.

In the patterns that follow (as in most crochet patterns) the stitch size is measured over 4 inches (10cm) horizontally and vertically, counting both rows and stitches.

left The basic equipment required is a crochet hook, a blunt-ended sewing needle, and sharp scissors. The hooks shown left (top to bottom) show the sizes from size B/1 (2.00mm) to size H/8 (5.00mm).

right To test your stitch size (or gauge), make a piece about 5 inches (13cm) square in the required stitch, using the recommended yarn and hook size (bottom right). Count the number of rows and the number of stitches over the given measurement (usually 4in/10cm). If these accurately match those of the stitch size specified in your pattern, you can safely use the recommended hook size. But if you find that you get too many stitches, change to a size larger hook and try again. If you get too few stitches, change to a size smaller hook and try again. The difference one hook size larger or smaller will make to the stitch size in the sample, right, is shown top left and top right respectively.

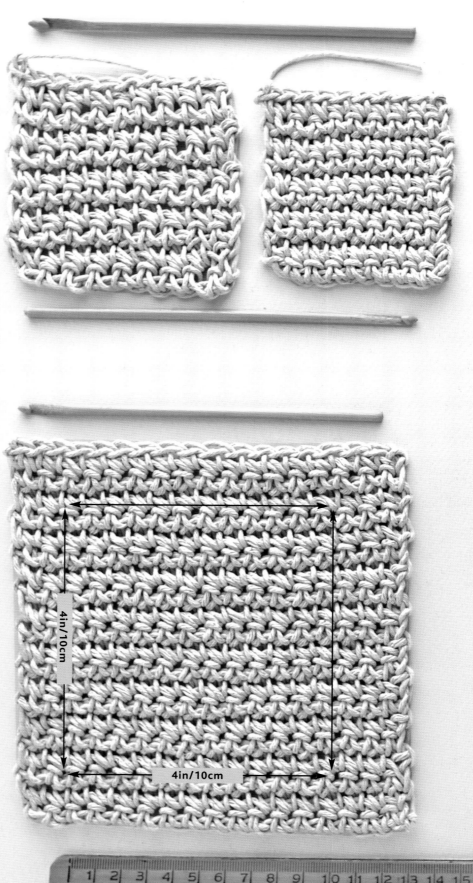

4in/10cm

4in/10cm

starting to crochet

To crochet easily and successfully, you need to hold the yarn and the hook comfortably, with enough tension on the yarn so that when you draw the hook around the yarn, it stays firmly in the lip of the hook. To this end, most people choose to wrap the yarn around their fingers, and some make an additional wrap around their little finger—choose whatever yarn-holding method that works best for you. Similarly, hold the hook in whatever way you find most comfortable. Some favor a pencil grip, while others hold the hook between their thumb and index finger like a knife. You may even prefer to change your grip depending on the type of stitch you are working at the time or on the size of the hook.

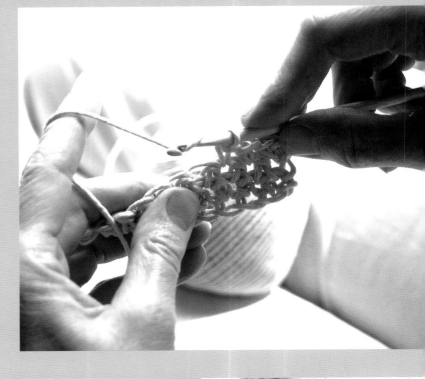

holding yarn/hook
method one

Wrap the ball end of the yarn around the little finger of your left hand, over the third finger, behind the second, and over the index finger. When you are starting to crochet, leave a long, loose tail end of yarn on the palm side of your hand. Hold the hook in your right hand like a pencil.

holding yarn/hook
method two

Wrap the ball end of the yarn between the little finger of your left hand, behind the third and second fingers, and over the index finger. When you are starting to crochet, leave a long, loose tail end of yarn on the palm side of your hand. Hold the hook in your right hand like you would a knife.

making the first loop

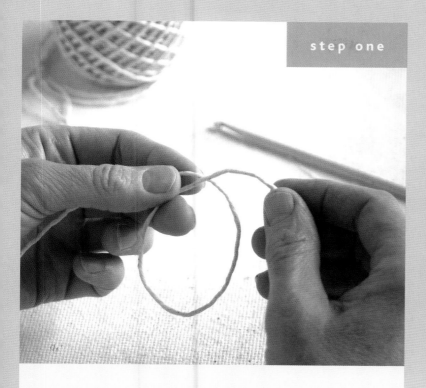

step one

To start to crochet, you first need to make a slip knot. There are many different ways in which you can do this, but the method shown below is very easy to follow. You can, of course, devise your own system if you prefer.

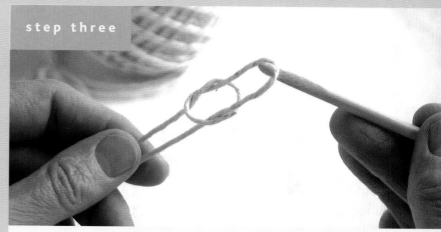

step three

one Make a loop in the tail end of the yarn as shown, crossing the tail end of the yarn over the ball end.

two Let the tail end drop down behind the loop, then pass the crochet hook over the loop on the right, catch it with the hook, and pull it through loop.

three Holding the tail end and the ball end of the yarn in your left hand, start to pull the hook in the opposite direction to create a loop on the hook.

four Keep pulling the yarn until the first loop forms on the hook, with a tight knot under it.

step two

step four

making a foundation chain

After you have made the slip knot on your hook, the next step is to create the foundation for the crochet fabric. This is called the "foundation chain." Your crochet instructions will tell you how many chains to make to start. Chain stitches are also used at the beginning of a row and for lace patterns.

step one

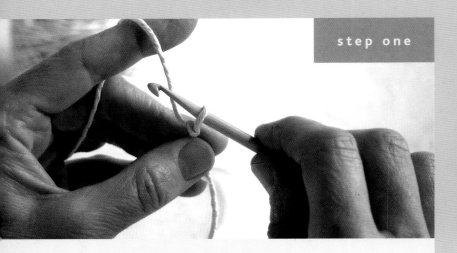

one   With the slip knot on the hook and the yarn held taut in your left hand, grip the tail end of the yarn. To begin the chain stitch, pass the tip of the hook in front of the yarn, then under and around it.

two   Keeping the yarn taut, catch the yarn in the lip of the hook, then draw it through the loop on the hook as indicated by the arrow.

step two

three   This completes the first chain and leaves you with a loop still on the hook. To make your next chain, pull a new loop through the loop on the hook. Keep the chain stitches slightly loose, as you will be working into them on your first row.

step three

four   Make the number of chains required. You should be able to count them easily, as each one makes a neat entity, with a visible smooth front, and more twisted back.

step four

Slip stitch is the shortest crochet stitch. If you work it into the foundation chain and continue making row after row of it, it forms a very dense, unyielding fabric. It is more commonly used to join the end and beginning of a round, or to work invisibly along the top of other stitches until you reach the required position.

three This completes the first slip stitch and leaves one loop on the hook. Work the next slip stitch into the next chain in the same way. If you intend to work into the slip stitches on the next row, then work them fairly loosely.

step three

step one

one Make a foundation chain (see previous page). Holding the end of the chain between the thumb and second finger of the left hand, and tensioning the yarn over the index finger of the left hand, insert the tip of the hook through the second chain from the hook as shown by the arrow.

two Catch the yarn with the hook (called "wrap the yarn over the hook") and draw it through the chain and the loop on the hook.

four Continue working a slip stitch in each chain to the end. To begin a second slip-stitch row, turn the work at the end of the first row. Then make one chain and work a slip stitch in the top of each stitch of the previous row.

step four

step two

single crochet

Single crochet is sometimes also known as "plain stitch." It creates a dense but still flexible fabric, which is ideal for hardwearing, strong textiles. The easiest of all crochet fabrics to make, it is used frequently in this book in an exciting range of yarn textures, including soft cotton yarn, rags, string, and leather. Single crochet and chain stitches can be combined to form other, softer fabrics.

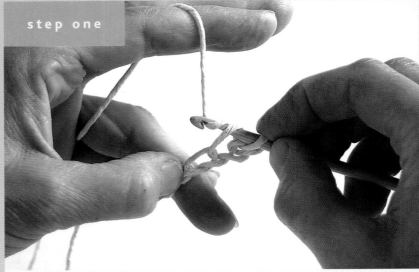

step one

one   Make your foundation chain. Then insert the hook through the second chain from the hook (see step 1 of slip stitch on previous page). Wrap the yarn over the hook as shown above and pull a loop through the chain.

two   There are now two loops on the hook. Wrap the yarn over the hook and pull a loop through both of these loops.

three   This completes the first stitch. To make the next stitch, insert the hook through the next chain, draw a loop through, then draw a loop through both loops on the hook.

four   Work a single crochet in each of the remaining chains in the same way to complete your first row.

second row

To start your second row of single crochet, turn the work so the loop on the hook is at the right edge. You will then have to make a "turning" chain to take the yarn up to the correct height.

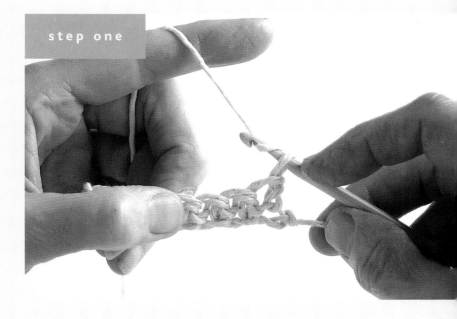

o n e At the beginning the second row, draw a loop through the loop on the hook to form a loose chain (called "chain 1").

t w o Inserting the hook under both loops at the top of the stitch, work a single crochet in each single crochet of the previous row. Work following rows in the same way as the second row.

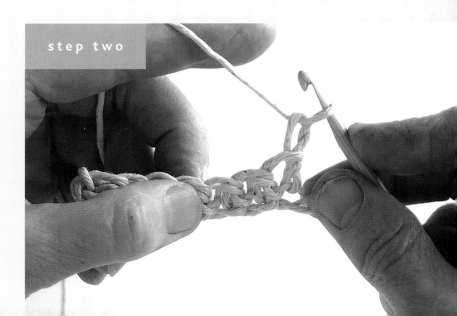

double crochet

A double crochet is taller than a single crochet. It results in a stitch that is more open and less dense, so it is a flexible, soft textile. It is worked in much the same way as single crochet, except that you wrap the yarn over the hook before beginning the stitch. And as it is taller, you begin the first row by working into the fourth chain from the hook.

step one

o n e   Make the number of foundation chains your require. Then wrap the yarn over the hook as shown and insert the hook into the fourth chain from the hook.

t w o   There are now three loops on the hook. Wrap the yarn over the hook and draw a loop through the first two loops on the hook (first arrow), leaving two loops on the hook. Next, wrap the yarn over the hook and draw it through the remaining two loops on the hook (second arrow).

t h r e e   This completes the first double crochet. Wrap the yarn over the hook to begin the second double crochet and work it into the next chain in the same way.

f o u r   Work a double in each chain to the end. Then turn the work to begin the next row. Make three chain (called "chain 3" or "ch3") at the beginning of the second row—this is the "turning" chain and counts as the first stitch of the row. Skip the first stitch in the row below and work the first double in the top of the next stitch. At the end of the row work the last stitch in the top of the chain-three (ch-3) at the edge. Work following rows as for the second.

1
2

half double & treble crochet

The two remaining basic crochet stitches are half doubles and trebles. A half double is slightly shorter than a double, and a treble slightly taller. Try them out following the instructions below, and you'll know all you need to know to work simple crochet pattern stitches!

half double

half double crochet Work in exactly the same way as double crochet, except in step 1 insert the hook into the third chain from the hook and in step 2 draw a single loop through all three loops on the hook to complete the stitch. In the second row work two turning chains instead of three.

treble crochet Work in exactly the same way as double crochet, except in step 1 wrap the yarn twice over the hook and insert the hook into the fifth chain from the hook, and in step 2 draw a loop through two loops on the hook three times instead of twice. In the second row work four turning chains instead of three.

treble

working in rounds

Some circular pieces require you to work in rounds rather than rows. The stitches may vary but the basic technique is the same. To begin, you will need to make a ring of a few chain stitches as the foundation. Yarn thickness will determine how many chains you make, but generally for a hole at the center that is closed, about four to six chains will do.

step three

three   Inserting you hook into the ring (not into the chain), work as many stitches into the ring as your instructions tell you. Catch the loose end of yarn into the stitches of the first round so you can use it to pull the hole tight later. When you work in rounds the right side is always facing you, so don't "turn" the work at the end of the round.

four   Before starting the second round of stitches, mark the beginning of the round—when working in rounds, it is sometimes hard to tell where one round ends and the next begins, so it is a good idea to position a marker here. Place a short length of a contrasting yarn across your crochet from front to back. Put it tight up against the loop on the hook as shown. When the second round is started the marker will be caught in postiton under the top of the first stitch and show you clearly where the round was begun. Pull out and reposition the marker at the end of each following round.

step one

one   Make six chains, then insert the hook through the first chain made. Wrap the yarn over the hook in the usual way, then draw a loop through the chain and the loop on the hook as for a slip stitch. This forms a ring of chains.

two   If you are working single crochet into the ring, start by making one chain. (Make three chains if your first round is doubles, two for half doubles, or four for trebles.)

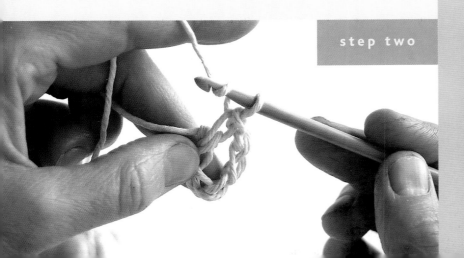

step two

step four

new yarns

If you want to start a new ball of yarn when the old one runs out, or when changing to a new color for stripes or for any other color pattern, there is no need to fasten off first. You can just keep crocheting and draw the new yarn in when it is needed. There's nothing to it!

step one

o n e   When working in single crochet, begin the stitch in the usual way by inserting the hook into the next stitch and drawing a loop through. Then drop the old yarn, pick up the new yarn, and wrap it over the hook. Draw a loop of the new yarn through the two loops on the hook to complete the single crochet. With other stitches, join in a new yarn in the same way—with the last loop of the stitch.

t w o   Work over the ends of the new and old yarn for several stitches, then neatly clip off the ends close to the fabric.

step two

finishing

Once you have completed a piece of work, you will need to fasten it to stop it from unraveling. This is also known as "casting off." To neaten your finished crochet pieces, weave all the loose ends of yarn into the fabric.

fastening off

fastening off

To fasten off, cut off the yarn leaving about 6inches (l5cm) or so. Then draw the loose end through the loop on the hook and pull tight.

weaving in

To weave in ends, thread the yarn into a blunt-ended needle with a suitably large eye, run the needle through several stitches near it, and then snip off the excess yarn.

weaving in

pillows

round pillow

The back and front of this simple, contemporary string pillow are worked round and round in a continuous, spiraling row of single crochet. To keep the pillow flat, you gradually build up the number of stitches in each round. It produces a firm, dense fabric.

making : the round pillow

PILLOW SIZE
Approximately 16in/40cm in diameter.

MATERIALS
4 x 98yd/89m balls thick kitchen twine
(from hardware or stationery stores)
Hook size F/5 (4.00mm)
Round pillow form 16in/40cm in diameter
(or customize a square one—see Tips)
Length of contrasting colored yarn for
marker

STITCH SIZE
This pillow has a "gauge" (stitch size)
of 15 stitches and 20 rows to 4in/10cm
measured over single crochet worked
in kitchen twine, but working to an exact
gauge is not essential (see Tips).

TECHNIQUES USED
Single crochet, working in rounds, and
joining in new balls of yarn.

TIPS
Working in rounds
When you work your crochet in rounds
you never have to turn the fabric. The right
side is always facing you.
Gauge
Don't worry about gauge too much!
Because this string pillow cover is made
in circles, you can just keep working
your stitches in a spiral until it is the
required size.
Marking the beginning of a round
Be sure to mark the beginning of each
round to make it easier to keep your place.
Joining in a new yarn
This technique is used for changing yarns
when your ball of yarn is finished or when
you want to start a new color for stripes.
Begin a single crochet in the usual way, by
drawing a loop through the next stitch,
then drop the old yarn and draw the new
yarn through both loops now on the hook

to finish the single crochet (see Crochet
Basics). Leave long loose ends of the old
and new yarns to weave in later, or work
over the ends of the old yarn for several
stitches before clipping them off.
Making a round pillow form
Customize a square pillow form to fit, by
first chalking a 16in/40cm circle on the
pillow. Then take each corner in turn, shake
the stuffing to the middle, fold down the
empty corners, and stitch through both
layers along the chalked line.

METHOD
Foundation-chain ring Leaving a long
loose end and using a size F/5 (4.00mm)
hook, chain 6 and join length of chain into
a ring by working a slip stitch into first
chain made.
Round 1 (right side) Chain 1, then
work 12sc into ring, working over long
loose end.

If you wish, you can make this simple pillow in a random color mix. The one shown right was worked in cotton in three colors: cream, beige, and green. To create a similar pillow, simply follow the pattern, and work in the new yarns randomly to create this informal effect, following the instructions on page 27 for joining in new yarn. If you wish to create a pillow with regular circular stripes, add the new colors at the start of each appropriate round. You could vary the thickness of the stripes, and the colors, to suit your own design.

Before starting the next round, place a short length of a contrasting yarn across your crochet fabric from front to back, tight up against the loop on the hook and above the working yarn. Then start to work the single crochet of *round 2*, catching the marker in position. The marker will show you where the round started, as it will be caught under the top of the first stitch of the round.

Round 2 (right side) 1sc in each of 12sc of previous round, making sure you are no longer working over loose end. At the end of each round pull the marker out and place it across your crochet fabric, up against the loop on the hook as before, so it will always be under the top of the first stitch of the round showing you where to start the next round.

Round 3 Work 2sc in each sc to end. There are now 24sc in the circle.

Round 4 Work 1sc in each sc to end.

Round 5 1sc in first sc, 2sc in next sc, *1sc in next sc, 2sc in next sc, repeat from * to end. 36sc.

Rounds 6 and 7 As round 4.

Round 8 1sc in each of first 2sc, 2sc in next sc, *1sc in each of next 2sc, 2sc in next sc, repeat from * to end. 48sc.

Rounds 9 and 10 As round 4.

Round 11 1sc in each of first 3sc, 2sc in next sc, *1sc in each of next 3sc, 2sc in next sc, repeat from * to end. 60sc.

Rounds 12 and 13 As round 4.

Round 14 1sc in each of first 4sc, 2sc in next sc, *1sc in each of next 4sc, 2sc in next sc, repeat from * to end. 72sc.

Continue in this way, working two rounds without increases followed by one round with 12 evenly spaced increases, until circle measures 16in/40cm across (about 40 rounds).

Slip stitch into next stitch and fasten off. Work another circle the same.

TO FINISH

Pull the long loose end at the center of each circle to tighten up the hole and weave it in on the wrong side of the work. Weave in any other loose ends on the wrong side as well.

Lay the circles out flat, then steam and press lightly.

Sew the circles together, or join with single crochet as follows:

Join the circles with sc

Place the circles together with the wrong sides facing each other, line up the stitches along the outside edge, and pin. Work 1sc through a sc at the edge of the two layers. Continue like this, working 1sc through each sc and making sure you catch in both layers with each stitch. When the opening is just large enough to insert the pillow form, push it inside and finish the edging. Fasten off and weave in the end.

chevron
pillow

This pillow is a reinvention of a popular sixties pattern. You can try out different colorways or group the stripes in varying pattern widths. The pillow is worked in bands of contrasting colors with a splash of metallic thread, but it looks good, too, when worked in a single color. Combine several plain or patterned versions to add a touch of glamour to a plain sofa or armchair.

PILLOW SIZE
Approximately 15¾in/40cm square.

MATERIALS
Rowan *Cotton Glacé* or a similar medium-weight mercerized cotton yarn (see page 122) in 4 contrasting colors as follows:
Color A: 2 x 1¾oz/50g balls in terracotta
Color B: 2 x 1¾oz/50g balls in off-white
Color C: 2 x 1¾oz/50g balls in rose pink
Color D: 1 x 1¾oz/50g ball in burgundy
Rowan *Lurex Shimmer* or a similar fine metallic yarn (see page 122) in one color as follows:
Color E: 1 x 1oz/25g ball in claret red
Hook size D/3 (3.00mm)
Pillow form 15¾in/40cm square

STITCH SIZE
This pillow has a "gauge" (stitch size) of 2 chevrons to 4½in/11.5cm and 9 rows to 4in/10cm measured over chevron pattern, but working to an exact gauge is not essential (see Tips).

TECHNIQUES USED
Double crochet, single crochet, working 3 doubles together, and joining in new balls of yarn.

TIPS
Gauge
Don't worry about gauge too much! If your pillow cover ends up a bit bigger or smaller, just buy a pillow form to fit.
Joining in a new yarn
This technique is used for changing yarns when your ball of yarn is finished or when you want to start a new color or texture. Change to the new yarn at the end of a row on the pillow. Begin the last double in the usual way, but change to the new yarn when drawing through the last loop of the stitch. Leave a long loose end of the old and new yarns to weave in later, or work over the ends for several stitches before clipping them off.

INSPIRATION
Experiment with different yarn textures or different color combinations, or try various widths of chevron stripes. For a pillow worked entirely in one color, just follow the instructions for the striped version, but work all 36 rows in the same color.

METHOD
Foundation chain Leaving a long loose end and using a size D/3 (3.00mm) hook and color A (terracotta), chain 74.
Row 1 Work 1dc into 4th ch from hook, *1dc in each of next 3ch, [yarn over hook and insert hook into next ch, yarn over hook and draw a loop through, yarn over hook and draw through first 2 loops on hook] 3 times, yarn over hook and draw

through all 4 loops on hook—this completes *3dc together*—, 1dc in each of next 3ch, 3dc in next ch, repeat from * to the end, but finishing with only 2dc in last ch instead of 3dc. Turn.

Row 2 Ch3, 1dc in first dc, *1dc in each of next 3dc, [yarn over hook and insert hook into next dc, yarn over hook and draw a loop through, yarn over hook and draw through first 2 loops on hook] 3 times, yarn over hook and draw through all 4 loops on hook—this completes *3dc together*—, 1dc in each of next 3dc, 3dc in next dc, repeat from * to end, but finishing last repeat with 2dc (instead of 3dc) in top of turning chain (instead of in a dc). Turn. Repeating *row 2*, work 2 rows more in color A.

Stripe pattern

Continuing to repeat *row 2* for chevron pattern, work 32 rows more in stripe pattern as follows:

Color B (off-white): 1 row.

Color E (metallic used double): 1 row.

Color B (off-white): 1 row.

Color C (rose pink): 2 rows.

Color D (burgundy): 2 rows.

Color A (terracotta): 2 rows.

Color D (burgundy): 2 rows.

Color B (off-white): 4 rows.

Color C (rose pink): 1 row.

Color B (off-white): 1 row.

Color C (rose pink): 4 rows.

Color E (metallic used double): 1 row.

Color A (terracotta): 4 rows.

Color B (off-white): 1 row.

Color D (burgundy): 1 row.

Color B (off-white): 1 row.

Color C (rose pink): 2 rows.

Color A (terracotta): 1 row.
Fasten off.
Make another piece the same.

TO FINISH

Weave in any loose ends on the wrong side of the work.

Lay the pieces out flat, then steam and press lightly.

Join the squares with sc

Place the two pieces together with the wrong sides facing each other, line up the stitches along the outside edge, and pin.

Work a single-crochet edging through both layers to join them. For an even edging, work 1sc between the stitches along the foundation-chain edge and along the last row; 2sc into each row end (around the double or turning chain) along the sides; and 3sc into each corner to keep the pieces square. Make sure you catch in both layers with each stitch, and when the opening is just large enough to insert the pillow form, push it inside and finish the edging.

Fasten off and weave in the end.

floor pillow

The ultimate in new crochet, this elegant floor pillow is
worked in leather. However, the design is so simple and
effective that any material could be used instead. Follow
the basic pattern principle—four large squares of single
crochet joined together to form a giant square. The textural
elegance of the design is enhanced by single-crochet seams
that are worked on the right side of the fabric to provide
a smart finishing touch. The crochet top is stitched to a
toning velvet pillow casing.

PILLOW SIZE

The crochet top is approximately 27in/
68cm square. (The pillow is approximately
27in/68cm square by 3³/4in/9.5cm deep.)

MATERIALS

9 x 55yd/50m balls 2mm-thick round
leather thronging or alternative yarn
Hook sizes L/11 (8.00mm) and N/13
(9.00mm)
1³/4yd/1.5m cotton velvet 44in/112cm
wide and matching sewing machine thread
Zipper (optional)
Pillow form to fit (see size above)
Strong sewing thread

STITCH SIZE

This pillow has a "gauge" (stitch size)
of 8 stitches and 10 rows to 4in/10cm
measured over single crochet, but working
to an exact gauge is not essential.
Each square of single crochet measures
about 13¹/4in/33cm square.

TECHNIQUES USED

Single crochet and joining in new balls
of yarn.

TIPS

Gauge

Don't worry about gauge too much!
Because this is a pillow, making it to an
exact size is not important. Just make sure
the four patches are square and complete
the crocheted top first, then make the
fabric pillow cover to fit it.

Joining in a new yarn

This technique is used for starting a new
ball of yarn when the one you are using
runs out. Begin a single crochet in the
usual way, by drawing a loop through the
next stitch, then drop the old yarn and
draw the new yarn through both loops
now on the hook to finish the single
crochet (see Crochet Basics). Leave a long
loose end of the old and new yarns to
weave in later, or work over the ends for
several stitches before clipping them off.

Leather

Leather thonging is available at craft
stores or from leather merchants. It is
quite hard on the hands, so concentrate
on one stitch at a time, as a unique aspect
of constructing a special textile. Warm the
leather in your hands as you work to

soften it. It can be a little sticky, too, and
a little talcum powder on the hook may
assist to pull it through.

Ready-made pillow

There are instructions for making your
own velvet pillow cover, but if you like, buy
a ready-made, covered pillow and make
your crochet top to fit it.

INSPIRATION

Use string or chunky felted yarn for less
expensive yet equally effective alternatives.
Work a little gauge swatch (see Crochet
Basics) to find out how many stitches and
rows you need.

METHOD

Square (make 4)

Foundation chain Leaving a long loose
end and using a size N/13 (9.00mm) hook
and leather thonging, chain 26.
Change to a size L/11 (8.00mm) hook and
begin working in single crochet as follows:
Row 1 Work 1sc into 2nd chain from hook,
1sc in each of remaining chains. Turn.
Row 2 Ch1 (this counts as first sc of row,
so work it loosely), skip first sc and work

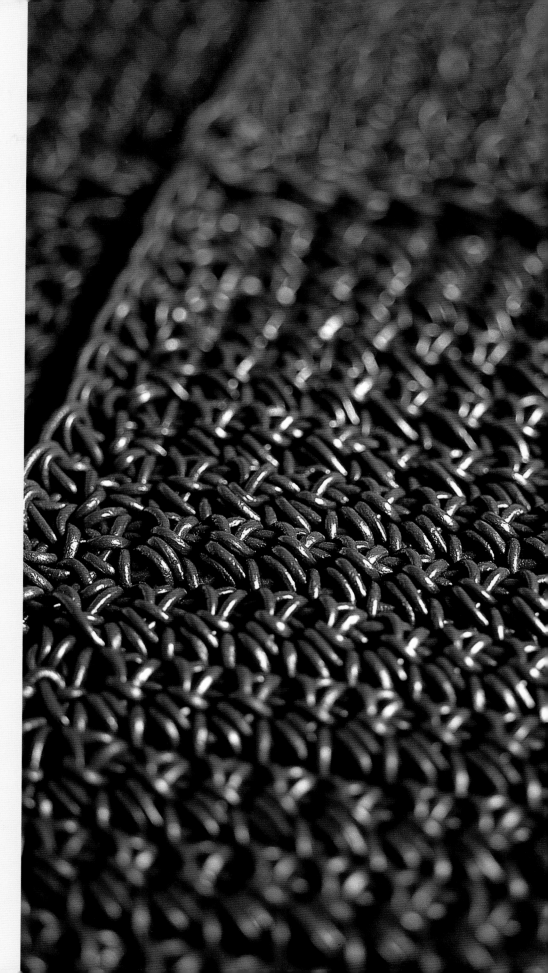

1sc in next sc, then work 1sc in each of remaining sc, work last sc in ch-1 at edge. Turn. There are 26 stitches in the row. Repeat *row 2* until work measures 13¼in/ 33cm from foundation-chain edge—a total of about 33 rows from beginning. Fasten off.

TO FINISH

Weave any loose ends into work.
Arrange the four crocheted pieces on a flat surface so that they form a large square, with the direction of the rows changing on every alternate square.
Using a size L/11 (8.00mm) hook and leather, join the squares together with single crochet on the right side of the fabric.

Edging

With the right side facing and using a size L/11 (8.00mm) hook and leather, work a row of sc all around the outside of the finished square. For an even edging, work 1sc in each foundation chain or stitch top; 1sc into each row end; and 3sc into each corner to keep the piece square. Fasten off.

FABRIC COVER

From the cotton velvet fabric, cut two pieces 28¼in/71cm square and four pieces 5in/12.5cm by 28¼in/71cm.
With the right sides together and stitching ⅝in/1.5cm from the edge, stitch the pieces together to make a "box"—the two large squares form the top and bottom and the smaller oblongs the four sides— leaving one of the long side seams open. Turn the cover right side out. If desired, insert a zipper in the opening. Otherwise, insert the pillow form and join the seam. Attach the crocheted leather square to the top of the cover with strong thread.

textured pillow

This pillow represents a sophisticated twist on a traditional pattern. Metallic yarns are used to create a simple contemporary textile for modern interiors. The pillow front is worked in a lacy stitch that is much easier to crochet than it looks, and the back is worked in plain single crochet. Work several pillows in different types of yarn to create a beautiful textural statement that works equally well on an ultra-modern couch or an antique leather armchair. You could create contrasts with completely different textures, such as suede, velvet, or string, if you prefer.

PILLOW SIZE

Approximately 17¼in/43cm square.

MATERIALS

11 x 1oz/25g balls Rowan *Lurex Shimmer* or a similar metallic yarn (see page 122) Hook sizes D/3 (3.00mm) and E/4 (3.50mm) Covered pillow 18in/45cm square

STITCH SIZE

The pillow front has a "gauge" (stitch size) of 5½ V-stitches and 10 rows to 4in/10cm measured over V-stitch pattern. The pillow back has a "gauge" (stitch size) of 22 stitches and 30 rows measured over single crochet (see Tips).

TECHNIQUES USED

Double crochet, working into a chain space, single crochet, and joining in new balls of yarn.

TIPS

Gauge

Don't worry about gauge too much! If your pillow front ends up a bit bigger or smaller than the size given here, just adjust the size of the single-crochet back pieces to suit it and buy a pillow to fit.

Joining in a new yarn

This technique is used for joining in a new ball of yarn when the one you are using runs out. Begin your double in the usual way, but change to the new ball of yarn when drawing through the last loop of the stitch. Leave a long loose end of the old yarn and the new yarn to weave in later.

Tightening the back opening

Be sure to change to a size smaller hook before working the last 1in/2.5cm of each back piece. This "snaps up" the edges and keeps them firm and even.

Buying a covered pillow

For a subtle effect, buy a covered pillow that closely matches the color of your chosen yarn. If you are good at sewing, you can buy a pillow form and cover it with a fabric of your choice.

INSPIRATION

Experiment with various colors and yarn textures, such as silk, ribbon, or linen. Different yarns will give different stitch sizes, so just adjust the number of foundation chains to get the size you want. The cluster pattern needs a multiple of 9 foundation chains plus 3 extra.

METHOD

Front

Foundation chain Leaving a long loose end and using a size E/4 (3.50mm) hook, chain 111.

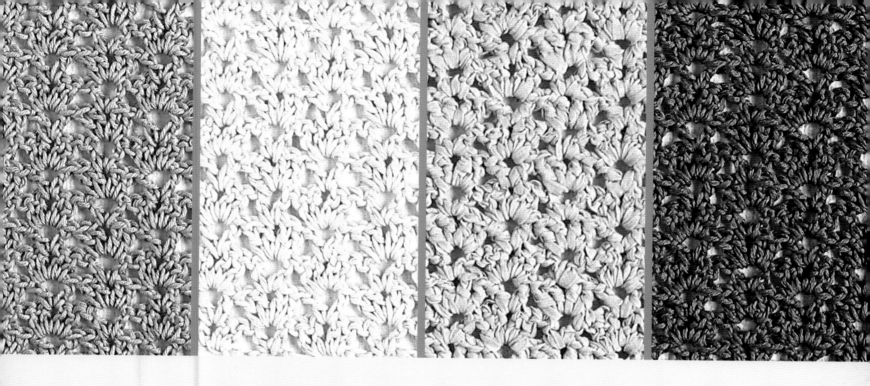

Row 1 Work 2dc into 5th chain from hook, ch1, 2dc in next ch, skip 3ch, [1dc, ch2, 1dc] all in next ch, *skip 3ch, 2dc in next ch, ch1, 2dc in next ch, skip 3ch, [1dc, ch2, 1dc] all in next ch, repeat from * to last 2ch, skip 1ch, 1dc in last ch. Turn.

Row 2 Ch3 to count as first dc, [2dc, ch1, 2dc] in first ch-2 space (inserting hook *under* the chain—not *into* the chain—when working the doubles), [1dc, ch2, 1dc] in next ch-1 space, *[2dc, ch1, 2dc] in next ch-2 space, [1dc, ch2, 1dc] in next ch-1 space, repeat from * to last 2dc, skip these 2dc, 1dc in next ch (top of turning chain). Turn. There are 24 V-stitches across the row (twelve 2dc V-stitches and twelve 4dc V-stitches).

Repeat *row 2* until pillow front measures 17¼in/43cm from foundation-chain edge (a total of about 43 rows from beginning). Fasten off.

Back (worked in 2 pieces)

Foundation chain Leaving a long loose end and using a size E/4 (3.50mm) hook, chain 96.

Row 1 Work 1sc into 2nd chain from hook, 1sc in each of remaining chains. Turn. There are 95sc in the row.

Row 2 Ch1, 1sc in each sc to end. Turn. Repeat *row 2* until the work measures 9½in/24cm from foundation-chain edge. Change to a size D/3 (3.00mm) hook and work 1in/2.5cm more in sc.

Fasten off.

Make a second piece the same.

TO FINISH

Weave any loose ends into the work. Lay the pieces out flat, then steam and press lightly.

Place back pieces on a flat surface and overlap two of the long edges by about 3¾in/10cm so that the pieces form a pillow back 17¼in/43cm square. Then place the pillow front on top (there is no right or wrong side to the front or the back pieces). Carefully pin the front to the backs around the outside edge, easing in the front to fit if necessary. Join the seam with overcast stitches, or with single crochet.

Turn the cover right side out and insert the covered pillow.

filet pillow

Filet, from the French word for net, is basically two simple stitches—chains and doubles—which are combined to create a square mesh, with some spaces in the mesh filled to form a motif or pattern. The simple lace look suits both traditional or contemporary interiors. A beautiful classic in pure white cotton, this pillow cover is very easy to make: the front is made up of nine squares of filet crochet joined together and finished with a picot edging to enhance its simplicity; the back is a piece of antique white linen.

making : the filet pillow

PILLOW FRONT SIZE

Approximately 15³/4in/39cm square, excluding the picot edging.

MATERIALS

4 x 1³/4oz/50g balls white Rowan *4ply Cotton* or a similar lightweight white cotton yarn (see page 122)
Hook size E/4 (3.50mm)
Pillow form 16in/40cm square
1yd/50cm of 44in/112cm wide white linen or cotton fabric and white sewing thread (see Tips)

STITCH SIZE

This pillow has a "gauge" (stitch size) of 13 spaces and 13 rows to 4in/10cm measured over filet crochet pattern. Each finished filet motif measures 5¼in/13cm square, but working to an exact gauge is not essential (see Tips).

TECHNIQUES USED

Filet crochet, working with charts, joining motifs together, and picot edge trimming.

TIPS

Gauge

Don't worry about gauge too much! If your pillow front ends up a bit bigger or smaller than the size given here, just adjust the size of the fabric cover to fit.

Joining in a new yarn

If your ball of yarn runs out while you are making one of the filet squares, join in a new one at the end of a row. Begin the last double of the row in the usual way, but change to the new ball of yarn when drawing through the last loop of the stitch. Leave a long loose end of the old yarn and the new yarn to weave in later.

Buying a pillow form

If you can't find a pillow form the exact size you need, buy one that is slightly larger rather than slightly smaller so that it puffs up the cover nicely.

Fabric pillow cover

There are instructions for making your own fabric pillow cover, but if you like, you can buy a ready-made plain white covered pillow and stitch your crochet to it.

Filet crochet charts

Filet crochet instructions are usually charted. The blank squares on the chart represent "spaces" in the filet and the squares with a symbol in them represent the solid "blocks" of doubles. To follow a filet chart, read the odd-numbered rows from right to left and the even-numbered rows from left to right. From this basic filet technique many different patterns can be designed.

INSPIRATION

Experiment with different weights of yarn, colors, and patterns to give a modern twist to the traditional. Use one motif as an insert in a linen bag or join three squares in a strip and use them as an edging on a velvet or satin pillowcase for a contemporary boudoir or guest room.

METHOD

Foundation chain Leaving a long loose end and using a size E/4 (3.50mm) hook, chain 38.

Row 1 Work 1dc into 6th chain from hook to make first "space," *ch1, skip 1ch, 1dc in next ch, repeat from * to end. Turn. There are 17 "spaces" in the row.

Row 2 Ch4 to count as first dc and first ch-1 space, skip first dc and first ch-1 space, *1dc in next dc, 1dc in next ch-1 space (inserting hook *under* the chain—not *into* the chain—when working the dc), repeat from * to last dc, 1dc in last dc, ch1, skip 1ch, 1dc in next ch (top of turning chain). Turn.

Row 3 Ch4 to count as first dc and first ch-1 space, skip first dc and first ch-1 space, 1dc in each of next 5dc (this makes one "filet space" followed by 2 "filet blocks"), [ch1, skip next dc, 1dc in next dc] 5 times (this makes 5 "spaces"), 1dc in each of next 2dc (this makes one "block"), [ch1, skip next dc, 1dc in next dc] 5 times

(this makes 5 more "spaces"), 1dc in each of next 4dc (this makes 2 "blocks"), ch1, skip next ch, 1dc in next ch (this makes one last "space"). Turn.

Row 4 Ch4, skip first dc and first ch-1 space, 1dc in each of next 3dc, ch1, skip 1dc, [1dc in next dc, 1dc in next ch-1 space] 3 times, 1dc in next dc, ch1, skip next ch-1 space, 1dc in next dc, 1dc in next ch-1 space, 1dc in each of next 3dc, 1dc in next ch-1 space, 1dc in next dc, ch1, skip next ch-1 space, [1dc in next dc, 1dc in next ch-1 space] 3 times, 1dc in next dc, ch1, skip 1dc, 1dc in each of next 3dc, ch1, skip next ch, 1dc in next ch. Turn.

Row 5 Ch4, skip first dc, 1dc in each of next 3dc, [ch1, 1dc in each of next 7dc] 3 times, ch1, 1dc in each of next 3dc, ch1, skip next ch, 1dc in next ch. Turn.

Row 6 Ch4, skip first dc, 1dc in each of

next 3dc, ch1, 1dc in each of next 7dc, 1dc in next ch-1 space, 1dc in next dc, ch1, skip next dc, 1dc in each of next 3dc, ch1, skip next dc, 1dc in next dc, 1dc in next ch-1 space, 1dc in each of next 7dc, ch1, 1dc in each of next 3dc, ch1, skip next ch, 1dc in next ch. Turn.

When working the next row, watch the chart as you make the "spaces" and "blocks"—you will see that each space on the chart is made up of a chain with a double on each side and each block is made by working a double where the chain would have been in the filet mesh. (See Tips for reading chart.)

Row 7 Ch4, skip first dc, 1dc in each of next 3dc, ch1, 1dc in next dc, [ch1, skip next dc, 1dc in next dc] twice, 1dc in each of next 4dc, ch1, 1dc in next dc, ch1, skip next dc, 1dc in next dc, ch1, 1dc in each of

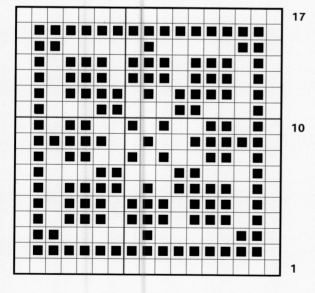

17

10

1

KEY

 = space

■ = block

next 5dc, [ch1, skip next dc, 1dc in next dc] twice, ch1, 1dc in each of next 3dc, ch1, skip next ch, 1dc in next ch. Turn. Continue forming the pattern with "blocks" and "spaces" in this way, and following the chart for the pattern, until row 17 has been completed. Fasten off. Work a total of 9 squares.

TO FINISH

Weave in any loose ends on the wrong side of the work.

Lay the nine pieces out flat, then steam and press lightly.

Overcast stitch the squares together.

Picot edging

For a detailed finish, work a simple picot-stitch edging all around the square. Begin by joining the yarn to a corner of the filet patchwork with a slip stitch. Then work the edging round and round the edge as follows:

Round 1 Ch4 to count as first dc and first ch-1 space, [ch1, 1dc] twice into same corner, then repeat [ch1, 1dc] evenly all around the edge, working the double into each double along the top and bottom, and into the top of each row end along the sides, and working [ch1, 1dc] 3 times into each of remaining three corners; at end of round, join with a slip stitch to 3rd of first ch-4.

Round 2 Ch1, 1sc in same place as slip stitch, 1sc in each ch-1 space (inserting hook *under* the chain—not *into* the chain—when working a sc in a ch-1 space) and 1sc in each sc to end of round; join with a slip stitch to first sc.

Round 3 Ch1, 1sc in same place as slip stitch, 1sc in each sc to end of round; join with a slip stitch to first sc.

Round 4 Ch1, [1sc, ch5, 1sc] all in same place as slip stitch to form first *picot*, 1sc in next sc, *[1sc, ch5, 1sc] all in next sc, 1sc in next sc, repeat from * to end; join with a slip stitch to first sc.

Fasten off.

FABRIC COVER

Cut your piece of white fabric to 17in/42cm by 40 1/4in/101cm. Begin the cover by making a hem along each of the two short edges. Fold 1/2in/1.5cm, then 1 1/2in/4cm to the wrong side and pin. Baste, then topstitch these two hems. Remove the basting and press. Lay the piece on a flat surface with the right side facing upward. Fold each hemmed edge toward the center and overlap them by 4 3/4in/12cm so that the cover measures 15 3/4in/39cm from fold to fold. Pin the open sides together and baste. Sew the seams 5/8in/1.5cm from the raw edges. Trim the seams and finish the raw edges with a zigzag stitch. Remove the basting, turn right side out, and press.

Hand-stitch the crochet piece to the front of the fabric cover, stitching around the edge of the filet-square patchwork and leaving the picot edging free.

throws

pieced throw

The effect of this throw is like a traditional "strippy" patchwork, worked in long strips that are then joined together. Each strip is in half double crochet in blocks of color—natural ecru with brilliant shades of pink and orange. The colors are staggered on each strip to produce a patchwork pattern. After the strips are crocheted together, they are finished with an edging of pink. As it is made in cotton, this throw is cool in summer and warm in winter. Great for bedroom or living room, it can be laundered time after time.

making : the pieced throw

THROW SIZE

Approximately 42³/₄in x 56in/107cm x 138cm, including edging.

MATERIALS

Rowan *Handknit DK Cotton* or a similar medium-weight yarn (see page 122) in 3 contrasting colors as follows:

Color A: 8 x 1³/₄oz/50g balls pink

Color B: 12 x 1³/₄oz/50g balls ecru

Color C: 6 x 1³/₄oz/50g balls orange

Hook sizes F/5 (4.00mm) and G/6 (4.50mm)

STITCH SIZE

This throw has a stitch size of 14 stitches and 11¹/₂ rows to 4in/10cm measured over half double crochet.

Each of the 10 strips of crochet is 5¹/₂in/13.5cm wide by 41³/₄in/104cm long, but working to an exact gauge is not essential (see Tips).

TECHNIQUES USED

Half double crochet, single crochet, and joining in new balls of yarn.

TIPS

Gauge

Don't worry about gauge too much! Because this is a throw, an exact width is not that important and you can make it any length you want by adding to or subtracting from the number of rows worked.

Starting each strip

The foundation chain of each strip is worked with a larger hook, so that the starting edge is not too tight and so that it is easier to work the crochet edging into it.

Joining in a new yarn

This technique is used for changing yarns when your ball of yarn is finished or when you want to start a new color for stripes. Change to the new yarn at the end of a row. Begin the last half double in the usual way, by wrapping the yarn over the hook, inserting the hook into the ch-2 at the end of the row and drawing a loop through; then drop the old yarn/color and draw the new yarn/color through all 3 loops now on the hook to finish the half double crochet.

Leave long loose ends of the old and new yarns to weave in later, or work over the ends for several stitches before clipping them off.

METHOD

Strip 1

Foundation chain Leaving a long loose end and using a size G/6 (4.50mm) hook and color A (pink), chain 20.

Change to a size F/5 (4.00mm) hook and begin the half double crochet as follows:

Row 1 Work 1hdc into 3rd chain from hook, 1hdc in each of remaining chains. Turn.

Row 2 Ch2 (this counts as first hdc of row, so work it loosely), skip first hdc and work 1hdc in next hdc, then work 1hdc in each of remaining hdc, work last hdc in ch-2 at edge. Turn. There are 19 stitches in the row.

Repeating *row 2*, work 14 rows more in color A (pink).

Continuing in hdc throughout, work 16 rows B (ecru), 16 C (orange), 16 B (ecru),

This throw would work equally well in wool or other soft-textured yarns. For a more vibrant design, the color blocks could be worked in a simple, regular stripe pattern like the one shown left or in alternating solid-colored and striped blocks. Random stripe patterns such as the one on the right give a modern and fresh look when combined with ecru, and would look equally stylish in combination with black.

16 A (pink), 16 B (ecru), 16 C (orange), and 8 B (ecru). Fasten off.

The 9 following strips are worked in the same stripe sequence, but started 8 rows later in the sequence as follows:

Strip 2

Work as for strip 1, but change the stripe sequence to 8 rows A (pink), 16 B (ecru), 16 C (orange), 16 B (ecru), 16 A (pink), 16 B (ecru), 16 C (orange), and 16 B (ecru).

Strip 3

Work as for strip 1, but change the stripe sequence to16 rows B (ecru), 16 C (orange), 16 B (ecru), 16 A (pink), 16 B (ecru), 16 C (orange), 16 B (ecru), and 8 A (pink).

Strip 4

Work as for strip 1, but change the stripe sequence to 8 rows B (ecru), 16 C (orange), 16 B (ecru), 16 A (pink), 16 B (ecru), 16 C (orange), 16 B (ecru), and 16 A (pink).

Strip 5

Work as for strip 1, but change the stripe sequence to 16 rows C (orange), 16 B (ecru), 16 A (pink), 16 B (ecru), 16 C (orange), 16 B (ecru), 16 A (pink), and 8 B (ecru).

Strip 6

Work as for strip 1, but change the stripe sequence to 8 rows C (orange), 16 B (ecru), 16 A (pink), 16 B (ecru), 16 C (orange), 16 B (ecru), 16 A (pink), and 16 B (ecru).

Strip 7

Work as for strip 1, but change the stripe sequence to 16 rows B (ecru), 16 A (pink), 16 B (ecru), 16 C (orange), 16 B (ecru), 16 A (pink), 16 B (ecru), and 8 C (orange).

Strip 8

Work as for strip 1, but change the stripe sequence to 8 rows B (ecru), 16 A (pink), 16 B (ecru), 16 C (orange), 16 B (ecru), 16 A (pink), 16 B (ecru), and 16 C (orange).

Strips 9 and 10

Work as for strips 1 and 2.

TO FINISH

Weave in any loose ends at the back of the work.

Lay each strip out flat, then steam and press lightly.

Arrange the bands side by side in the order in which they were made (from right to left), with all the foundation-chain edges at the bottom. (Joined in this order, the blocks of colors will form diagonal stripes across the throw.) Join the strips together with overcast stiches; or by holding the pieces with right sides together and working a row of sc in color B (ecru) through both thickness (1sc per row end).

Edging

Using a size F/5 (4.00mm) hook and color A (pink), work a row of single crochet around the edge of the throw. For an even edging, work 1sc in each chain along the foundation-chain edge; 1sc in each sc along the top; 1sc into each row end along the sides; and 3sc into each corner to keep the corners square.

Fasten off and weave in end.

textured throw

A timeless classic, this simple textured throw is an updated version of a traditional waffle blanket. It is worked in the simplest of textural stitches and bordered with a band of single crochet. Crocheted in a beautiful, matte, neutral, stone-colored linen yarn, this throw is both sophisticated and modern. Use it anywhere—in the house, the garden, or the car.

making : the textured throw

THROW SIZE
Approximately 49¼in x 61¾in/123cm x 154cm.

MATERIALS
29 x 1¾oz/50g balls Rowan *Linen Drape* or a similar lightweight linen yarn (see page 122)
Hook size E/4 (3.50mm)

STITCH SIZE
This throw has a "gauge" (stitch size) of 6½ V-stitches and 8½ rows to 4in/10cm measured over V-stitch pattern, but working to an exact gauge is not essential (see Tips).

TECHNIQUES USED
Double crochet, working into a chain space, single crochet, working a border in rounds, and joining in new balls of yarn.

TIPS
Gauge and throw size
Don't worry about gauge too much!

Because this is a throw, an exact size is not that important as long as it suits your purposes and the fabric is soft and supple. You can make the throw to any length you want by working more or fewer rows. You can also alter the width by adding to or subtracting from the number of V-stitches across the row. Make 3 foundation chains for every V-stitch you need—then work 3 extra foundation chains before starting *row 1*.

Joining in a new yarn
This technique is used for starting a new ball of yarn when the one you are using runs out or when working stripes. Begin your double in the usual way, but change to the new ball of yarn when drawing through the last loop of the stitch. Leave a long loose end of the old yarn and the new yarn to weave in later.

INSPIRATION
Experiment with different yarn textures, such as lurex, suede, or fine merino wool.

METHOD
Foundation chain Leaving a long loose end and using a size E/4 (3.50mm) hook, chain 231.

Row 1 Work 1dc into 4th chain from hook, ch1, 1dc in next ch, *skip 1ch, 1dc in next ch, ch1, 1dc in next ch, repeat from * to last ch, 1dc in last ch. Turn.

Row 2 Ch3 to count as first dc, [1dc, ch1, 1dc] in first ch-1 space (inserting hook *under* the chain—not *into* the chain— when working the doubles), *[1dc, ch1, 1dc] in next ch-1 space, repeat from * to end, 1dc in top of turning chain. Turn. There are 76 V-stitches in the row. Repeat *row 2* until work measures 59¼in/148cm from foundation-chain edge (a total of about 126 rows from beginning). Fasten off.

TO FINISH
Weave any loose ends into the work. Lay the work out flat, then steam and press lightly.

Border

Using a size E/4 (3.50mm) hook, join
yarn to edge of throw with a slip stitch by
inserting hook through a chain near the
center of the foundation-chain edge of the
throw and drawing a loop through, then
work the border in rounds as follows:

Round 1 Ch1, 1sc in same place as
slip stitch was worked, 1sc in next ch,
then continue in sc around the entire
edge of the throw, working 1sc in each
foundation chain, 2sc into each row end
along the sides, 1sc in each stitch across
the last row, and 3sc into each corner;
join with a slip stitch to top of first sc
of round.

Round 2 Ch1, 1sc in same place as slip
stitch was worked, then work 1sc in each
sc along sides and 3sc in each center sc of
each 3sc-group at corners; join with a slip
stitch to top of first sc of round.

Work 5 rounds more as *round 2* for a
1¼in/3cm deep border.

Fasten off and weave in any remaining
loose ends.

modern afghan

This is a simple, easy project to make and it can be picked up whenever time allows. Traditional crochet afghan squares are worked in subtle toning colors of soft natural cotton, joined together to make a stylish throw for sofa or car, or even the basket of your much-loved dog or cat. Cotton washes well time and time again, so it is not only comfortable but practical, too. Each afghan square is worked in a combination of three of the colors, and they are joined together in a simple layout with the fourth color. The blend of neutral colors chosen gives this little afghan a modern twist, but, if you wish, you can make it from leftover yarns from other projects in a vibrant mix of colors.

making : the modern afghan

AFGHAN SIZE

Approximately 29 1/2in/75cm square.
(This small size is for your dog—to make
a bigger afghan, see Inspiration.)

MATERIALS

Rowan *Handknit DK Cotton* or a similar
medium-weight cotton yarn (see page
122) in 4 contrasting colors as follows:
Color A: 2 x 1 3/4oz/50g balls in off-white
Color B: 2 x 1 3/4oz/50g balls in dark taupe
Color C: 2 x 1 3/4oz/50g balls in black
Color D: 3 x 1 3/4oz/50g balls in light beige
Hook size D/3 (3.00mm)

STITCH SIZE

This afghan is made up of squares (made
in 4 rounds) that measure 4in/10cm by
4in/10cm, but working to an exact
"gauge" (stitch size) is not essential
(see Tips).

TECHNIQUES USED

Working afghan squares in rounds,
doubles, single crochet, joining squares
together, and working a simple border.

TIPS

Gauge

Don't worry about gauge too much!
Because this is an afghan, making it to
an exact size is not important.

Working in rounds

When you work your crochet in rounds
you never have to turn the fabric. The
right side is always facing you.

Joining in new colors

When starting a new color on your square
motif, leave a long loose end of the old
yarn and the new yarn to weave in later,
or make less work for yourself by working
over the yarn ends for several stitches
before clipping them off.

Squares edgings

For a nice crisp edge on the motif squares,
work the single crochet of the first round
of the squares edging into the back loop
of each stitch. Work the single crochet in
round 2 into both loops in the usual way.

Joining squares together

The easiest way to join the squares is
given in the instructions, but if you are an
experienced crocheter you can also join
them together with single crochet in the
way patchwork blocks are joined. To do
this, omit the squares edging and use color
D (light beige) to join the squares together
into 6 strips of 6 squares. Work 4 rows of
sc between the squares, joining them
together on the 4th row with right sides
facing. When you have joined squares into
6 strips, join the rows together in the same
way, working 4 rows of sc between them
and joining them together on the 4th row.
Then work the outer border in 4 rounds of
sc in color D (light beige) and the final
round in color C (black).

INSPIRATION

Experiment with different colors, and try
out different arrangements of the variously
colored squares. Use several colors or
simply two colors, or make all the
squares in a single color for a simple
but contemporary look. Vary the size
of the afghan to suit your personal
requirements—work larger squares or
more of them to make a larger afghan for
the living room or bedroom or car.

METHOD

The afghan is made up of 36 squares that are each worked in the round using 3 colors—A (off-white), B (dark taupe), and C (black). Work the first square as follows:

Foundation-chain ring Leaving a long loose end and using a size D/3 (3.00mm) hook and color A, chain 6 and join length of chain into a ring by working a slip stitch into first chain made.

Round 1 (right side) Using A, ch3, 2dc into ring, *ch3, 3dc into ring, repeat from * twice more, ch3; join with a slip stitch to 3rd of first ch-3.

Break off color A and fasten off.

Round 2 Using B, join on yarn with a slip stitch by inserting hook into any ch-3 space and drawing a loop through, ch3, [2dc, ch3, 3dc] in same space as slip stitch was worked, *ch1, [3dc, ch3, 3dc] in next ch-3 space, repeat from * twice more, ch1; join with a slip stitch to 3rd of first ch-3.

Break off color B and fasten off.

Round 3 Using C, join on yarn with a slip stitch by inserting hook into a ch-3 space and drawing a loop through, ch3, [2dc, ch3, 3dc] in same space as slip stitch was worked, *ch1, 3dc in next ch-1 space, ch1, [3dc, ch3, 3dc] in next ch-3 space, repeat from * twice more, ch1, 3dc in next ch-1 space, ch1; join with a slip stitch to 3rd of first ch-3.

Break off color C and fasten off.

Round 4 Using A, join on yarn with a slip stitch by inserting hook into a ch-3 space and drawing a loop through, ch3, [2dc, ch3, 3dc] in same space as slip stitch was worked, *[ch1, 3dc in next ch-1 space] twice, ch1, [3dc, ch3, 3dc] in next ch-3 space, repeat from * twice more, [ch1, 3dc in next ch-1 space] twice, ch1; join with a slip stitch to 3rd of first ch-3. Fasten off.

Make 5 more squares exactly the same. For the remaining 30 squares, vary the color sequence as follows:

Make 6 squares—round 1 color A; round 2 color C; round 3 color B; and round 4 color A.

Make 6 squares—round 1 color B; round 2 color A; round 3 color C; and round 4 color B.

Make 6 squares—round 1 color B; round 2 color C; round 3 color A; and round 4 color B.

Make 6 squares—round 1 color C; round 2 color A; round 3 color B; and round 4 color C.

Make 6 squares—round 1 color C; round 2 color B; round 3 color A; and round 4 color C.

TO FINISH

Weave any loose ends into the work.

Squares edging

Using a size D/3 (3.00mm) hook and color D (light beige), edge each square with 2 rounds of single crochet as follows:

Round 1 (right side) Join on yarn with a slip stitch by inserting hook into first chain of a ch-3 group at a corner and drawing a loop through, ch1, 1sc in same place as slip stitch was worked, 3sc in next ch (corner chain), 1sc in next ch, [1sc in each of next 3dc, 1sc in next ch-1] 3 times, 1sc in each of next 3dc, *1sc in first ch of next ch-3 group, 3sc in next ch, 1sc in next chain, [1sc in each of next 3dc, 1sc in next ch-1] 3 times, 1sc in each of next 3dc, repeat from * twice more; join with a slip stitch to top of first sc.

Round 2 Ch1, 1sc in same place as slip stitch was worked, 1sc in each sc along the sides and 3sc in each corner sc (the center sc of each 3-sc group); join with a slip stitch to top of first sc.
Fasten off.

Joining squares

Arrange motifs into 6 rows of 6 squares each so you have a good random mixture of the various colorways. Overcast stitch the squares together into 6 strips of 6 squares, then sew the strips together. Lay the work out flat, then steam and press lightly.

Outer border

Using a size D/3 (3.00mm) hook, work 3 rounds of single crochet around the outer edge of the afghan as follows:

Round 1 (right side) Using D (light beige), join on yarn with a slip stitch by inserting hook into a sc along one edge of afghan and drawing a loop through, ch1, 1sc in same place as slip stitch was worked, 1sc in each sc along the sides and 3sc in each corner sc (the center sc of each 3-sc group); join with a slip stitch to top of first sc.

Round 2 Still using D, ch1, 1sc in same place as slip stitch was worked, 1sc in each sc along the sides and 3sc in each corner sc (the center sc of each 3-sc group); join with a slip stitch to top of first sc.

Round 3 Using C (black), work as round 2. Fasten off.

Weave in any remaining loose ends.

stripy throw

Make this elegant throw for the sofa or for the car. It is worked in warm neutral colors with a beautiful cotton microfiber yarn that is lightweight and modern. The stitch pattern is a supple variation on basic single crochet and looks very effective in this simple repeating stripe pattern. The throw takes no time at all to crochet. It is lighter to work than knitting can be, so it's easy to pick up and put down.

making : the stripy throw

THROW SIZE
Approximately 33in x 55in/83cm x 138cm.

MATERIALS
Rowan *All Seasons Cotton* or a similar
medium-weight cotton yarn (see page
122) in 4 contrasting colors as follows:
Color A: 10 x 1³/₄oz/50g balls in brown
Color B: 5 x 1³/₄oz/50g balls in beige
Color C: 3 x 1³/₄oz/50g balls in lime
Color D: 2 x 1³/₄oz/50g balls in white
Hook size J/10 (6.00mm)

STITCH SIZE
This throw has a "gauge" (stitch size) of 15
stitches and 14¹/₂ rows to 4in/10cm

measured over stitch pattern, but
working to an exact gauge is not
essential (see Tips).

TECHNIQUES USED
Single crochet, working into a chain
space, and joining in new balls of yarn.

TIPS
Gauge
Don't worry about gauge too much!
Because this is a throw, an exact width
is not that important and you can
make it any length you want by adding
to or subtracting from the number of
rows worked.

Joining in a new yarn
This technique is used for changing yarns
when your ball of yarn is finished or when
you want to start a new color for stripes.
Change to the new yarn at the end of a
row. Begin the last single crochet in the
usual way, by drawing a loop through the
last chain space, then drop the old yarn
and draw the new yarn through both
loops now on the hook to finish the
single crochet (see Crochet Basics for
instructions on how to join in new yarn).
Leave long loose ends of the old and new
yarns to weave in later, or work over the
ends for several stitches before clipping
them off.

inspiration

If you wish, you can make a single-color version of this throw, which exposes the simple textural beauty of the stitch. Alternatively, you can give your throw a completely different look by changing the color scheme. Use varying shades of the same color for a smoothly blending effect, or starkly contrasting tones for a striking boldness. Broader or narrower stripes, or wide uniform bands of color, will also alter the effect. Before starting an original version, make a long thin strip to test your stripe creation.

METHOD

Foundation chain Leaving a long loose end and using a size J/10 (6.00mm) hook and color A (brown), chain 126.

Row 1 Work 1sc into 4th chain from hook, *ch1, skip 1ch, 1sc in next ch, repeat from * to end. Turn.

Row 2 Ch2 (this counts as first sc and first ch-1 space), skip first sc and work 1sc in first ch-1 space (inserting hook *under* the chain—not *into* the chain—when working the sc), *ch1, skip next sc, 1sc in next ch-1 space, repeat from * to end, working last sc in chain space at edge. Turn.

Repeating *row 2*, work 22 rows more in

pattern in color A (brown).

Stripe pattern repeat

Continuing to repeat *row 2* for stitch pattern, work next 42 rows in stripes as follows:

Color B (beige): 2 rows.
Color A (brown): 2 rows.
Color B (beige): 4 rows.
Color C (lime): 2 rows.
Color D (white): 2 rows.
Color C (lime): 2 rows.
Color D (white): 2 rows.
Color C (lime): 2 rows.
Color B (beige): 4 rows.
Color A (brown): 2 rows.
Color B (beige): 2 rows.

Color A (brown): 16 rows.
Work this 42-row stripe-pattern repeat 4 times in total.
Work 8 rows more in color A (brown), so that the throw ends with 24 rows A to match brown border at beginning.
Fasten off.

TO FINISH

Weave any loose ends into the work. Lay the work out flat, then steam and press lightly.

rag rug

This crocheted rag rug was created with simple natural linens and cottons in plain natural tones and in simple black and white patterns, including a ticking stripe and a gingham. You can make your own rug from scraps, recycled from worn-out or outgrown clothes, or various remnants. The fabric is simply cut up into thin strips of various lengths and crocheted together randomly with a large hook. Rag rugs work well in hallways or bathrooms, on flagstones or parquet. The ends of the rag strips can be woven into the crochet, or knotted and left sticking out for a textured effect.

making : the rag rug

RAG RUG SIZE
Approximately 26 1/2in x 35in/66.5cm x 87.5cm.

MATERIALS
Scraps of an assortment of fabric (the rug shown here was made from cotton/linen mixes in three natural shades, a black linen, a white linen, a cotton ticking with narrow black and white stripes, a black and white gingham, and a black and white check)
Hook size L/11 (8.00mm)

STITCH SIZE
This rug has a "gauge" (stitch size) of 7 1/2 stitches and 8 rows to 4in/10cm measured over single crochet, but working to an exact gauge is not essential (see Tips for more about gauge).

TECHNIQUES USED
Making yarns from fabric by cutting into strips, single crochet, and joining in new fabric strips.

TIPS
Gauge
Don't worry about gauge too much! Because this rug can be made to any size and is worked randomly, it doesn't matter what your gauge is as long as it produces a nice soft rug. If your stitches are so tight you find them difficult to work comfortably, try a larger hook size.

Cutting fabric strips
Before starting to crochet, cut some long strips from each of your fabrics. Make the strips about 5/8in/1.5cm wide and cut them on the straight grain of the fabric. If you like, you can roll the strips into balls

just like balls of ordinary yarn. When you run out of strips as you are crocheting, cut more as you need them.

Joining in a new strip
This technique is used for starting a new strip when the one you are using runs out or when changing to a new color for stripes. Begin a single crochet in the usual way, by drawing a loop through the next stitch, then drop the old strip and draw the new strip through both loops now on the hook to finish the single crochet (see Crochet Basics). Leave long loose ends of the old and new strips to weave in later, or work over the ends for several stitches before clipping them off.

METHOD
Foundation chain Leaving a long loose end and using a size L/11 (8.00mm) hook

Experiment with different fabric textures, but try to keep the strips to a similar width when cutting. Use different color tones or work regular stripes instead of random ones. Vary the size of the rug to suit your personal requirements—maybe a runner for a hallway—or work manageable sections or squares and sew them together to make a larger rug for the living room or bedroom. Use fabric strips in patterns, prints, and stripes of similar tones to create special effects. Try working in a spiral (as for the round pillow cover on pages 30–33) to create a circular rug.

and a plain natural-colored fabric strip, chain 50.

Row 1 Work 1sc into 2nd chain from hook, 1sc in each of remaining chains. Turn.

Joining in new strips of fabric at random for a random stripe effect, continue as follows:

Row 2 Ch1 (this counts as first sc of row, so work it loosely), skip first sc and work 1sc in next sc, then work 1sc in each of remaining sc, work last sc in ch-1 at edge. Turn. There are 50 stitches in the row.

Repeat *row 2* until rug measures approximately 35in/87.5cm from foundation-chain edge (a total of about 70 rows from beginning) or to the desired length.

Fasten off.

TO FINISH

Weave any loose ends into the single crochet.
Lay the work out flat, then steam and press lightly.

containers

boxes

These simple crocheted boxes have a variety of uses—to store shoes or jewelry, to stack cutlery in, or to display yarns and threads for projects; or put them to use in the bathroom. Have fun thinking up new combinations of colors and textures, and give the boxes as a gift, attractive and useful. They are worked in basic single crochet using kitchen twine, trimmed with cotton "rag" strips. Three different shapes and sizes are given here, but it is very easy to make them to suit your own requirements.

making : the boxes

BOX SIZES

Box A: The tall square box with orange trim measures 6in x 6in x 8 1/4in tall/15cm x 15cm x 20.5cm tall.

Box B: The small rectangular box with bright pink trim measures 10 3/4in x 4 1/4in x 3 1/4in tall/27cm x 10.5cm x 8cm tall.

Box C: The large rectangular box with pale pink trim measures 11 3/4in x 8 1/4in x 4 3/4in tall/29.5cm x 21cm x 12cm tall. *Note that the instructions are given for box A (the square box) and the figures for the two rectangular boxes are given in parentheses like this—box A (box B: box C).*

MATERIALS

4(2:5) x 44yd/40m balls thick kitchen twine (available from local hardware or stationery stores)
Fabric remnants for rag edging—in orange, bright pink, and pale pink
Hook sizes G/6 (4.50mm) and H/8 (5.00mm)

STITCH SIZE

These boxes have a "gauge" (stitch size) of 11 1/2 stitches and 13 rows to 4in/10cm measured over single crochet, but working to an exact gauge is not essential (see Tips).

TECHNIQUES USED

Single crochet, joining in new balls of yarn, and making yarn from fabric by cutting into strips.

TIPS

Gauge

Don't worry about gauge too much! Because the boxes can be made to any size, it doesn't matter what your gauge is as long as it produces a fairly stiff fabric that will hold its shape nicely. Just make the sides and ends of the boxes first, following the instructions given. Then make the base, adding to or subtracting from the number of rows recommended

until the depth of the piece matches the width of the ends.

Joining in a new yarn

This technique is used for starting a new ball of yarn when the one you are using runs out. Begin a single crochet in the usual way, by drawing a loop through the next stitch, then drop the old yarn and draw the new yarn through both loops now on the hook to finish the single crochet (see Crochet Basics). Leave a long loose end of the old and new yarns to weave in later, or work over the ends before clipping them off.

Cutting fabric strips

For the rag edging on the boxes, cut some long fabric strips about 5/8in/1.5cm wide and cut them on the straight grain of the fabric. If you like, you can roll the strips into balls just like balls of ordinary yarn. For a long continuous strip, cut along the first edge, then turn at the corner, cutting in a spiral toward the center.

inspiration

String (or twine) is a good material for
crochet boxes, but you could also try
using other textures and colors, or
make a whole box with rag strips in
various shades and in prints, stripes,
and patterns. Just work the single
crochet tightly to keep the fabric firm.
Use the boxes for storage—the ones
here create an attractive display on
the bathroom shelf.

METHOD

Box sides (make 2)

Foundation chain Leaving a long loose
end and using a size H/8 (5.00mm) hook
and twine, chain 17(31:34).

Row 1 Work 1sc into 2nd chain from
hook, 1sc in each of remaining chains.
Turn.

Row 2 Ch1 (this counts as first sc of row,
so work it loosely), skip first sc and work
1sc in next sc, then work 1sc in each of
remaining sc, work last sc in ch-1 at edge.
Turn. There are 17(31:34) stitches in
the row.

Repeat *row 2* until work measures
7¾(2¾:4¼)in/19(6.5:10.5)cm from
foundation-chain edge—a total of about
25(9:14) rows from beginning.
Fasten off.

Box ends (make 2)

Foundation chain Leaving a long loose
end and using a size H/8 (5.00mm) hook
and twine, chain 17(12:24).

Work *rows 1* and *2* as for box sides.
Repeat *row 2* on these 17(12:24) stitches
until there are same number of rows as
on sides.
Fasten off.

Box base (make 1)

Foundation chain Leaving a long loose
end and using a size H/8 (5.00mm) hook
and twine, make 17(31:34) chain.
Work *rows 1* and *2* as for box sides.
Repeat *row 2* on these 17(31:34) stitches
until work measures 6(4¼:8¼)in/
15(10.5:21)cm from foundation-chain
edge—a total of about 19(14:27) rows
from beginning.
Fasten off.

TO FINISH

Weave any loose ends into work.
Overcast stitch the ends and sides
together along the short seams to make a
box shape—the seams are meant to show
on the outside of the box, so hold the
pieces with the wrong sides together
when seaming.
Sew the box base to the sides and ends
in the same way.

"Rag" edging

Using a size G/6 (4.50mm) hook and
twine, work a row of sc all around the top
of the box. Fasten off.
Using a size G/6 (4.50mm) hook and a
orange (bright pink: pale pink) fabric strip
(see Tips), work another row of sc.
Fasten off. Sew in any loose ends.

string
bottle
cover

These sculptural containers have a strong architectural presence. Created in natural yarns—a combination of hemp and simple string—they are worked in basic single crochet. The covers have been designed to fit neatly over wine or mineral water bottles as decoration. Equally, an empty bottle can be used as a vase.

making : the string bottle cover

BOTTLE COVER SIZE
Approximately 17³/₄in tall/45cm.
See Tips for adjusting circumference to fit different bottle sizes.

MATERIALS
1 x large ball medium-weight brown string; and 2 x 44yd/40m balls thick natural-colored kitchen twine (both available from local hardware or stationery stores)
Hook size size I/9 (5.50mm)
Wine or water bottle
Two lengths of contrasting colored yarn or two safety pins for markers

STITCH SIZE
This bottle cover has a "gauge" (stitch size) of 10¹/₂ stitches and 11¹/₂ rows to 4in/10cm measured over single crochet using one strand of thick twine or 2 strands of medium-weight brown string, but working to an exact gauge is not essential (see Tips).

TECHNIQUES USED
Single crochet, working in rounds, simple decreases, and joining in new balls of yarn.

TIPS
Working in rounds
When you work your crochet in rounds you never have to turn the fabric. The right side is always facing you.
Bottle size and gauge
Don't worry about gauge too much!
A cover worked to the specified stitch size will easily fit a standard-size wine bottle or a big mineral-water bottle with plenty of room to spare, and the circumference of the cover is easy to alter. Work the first 3 rounds of the cover, then slip it over your bottle—it should slide on easily, with room left over. If you want a slightly snugger fit or if the cover it too tight, just start over, making the foundation chain a little shorter or a little longer.

Joining in a new yarn
This technique is used for changing yarns when your ball of yarn is finished or when you want to start a new color for stripes. Begin a single crochet in the usual way, by drawing a loop through the next stitch, then drop the old yarn and draw the new yarn through both loops now on the hook to finish the single crochet. Leave a long loose end of the old and new yarns to weave in later, or work over the ends for several stitches before clipping them off.

METHOD
Foundation-chain ring Leaving a long loose end and using a size I/9 (5.50mm) hook and 2 strands of medium-weight

Try using different string textures or different stripe combinations for your bottle covers. To make round baskets to go with your bottle covers, first work the circular bottom of the container following the instructions for the round string pillow on pages 30–33. When the circle is the diameter required for your basket, stop adding stitches. If you continue on this fixed number of stitches, the sides of the basket will begin to form. Fasten off when the basket is the desired height.

brown string together, chain 33 and join length of chain into a ring by working a slip stitch into first chain made.

Round 1 (right side) Chain 1, work 1sc in same chain as slip stitch was worked, 1sc in each of remaining 32ch. There are now 33sc in the round.

Round 2 (right side) Skip the slip stitch and the ch-1 and work 1sc in top of first sc of previous round, 1sc in each of the remaining 32sc of previous round. 33sc. Continue working these 33 stitches in rounds in a spiral until work measures 5in/13cm from foundation-chain edge. Change to one strand of thick kitchen twine and continue until work measures 9in/23cm from foundation-chain edge. (As the cover is being worked in a spiral there is no need to keep track of exactly where each new round begins and ends, so when the cover is 9in/23cm tall you can start

the next round in any place you choose.) Decrease 2 stitches in next round as follows:

Next round (decrease round) [Insert hook into next sc, yarn over hook and draw a loop through] twice, yarn over hook and draw through all 3 loops on hook—called *decrease one stitch*—, mark the decrease just made with a colored thread or a safetly pin, continue in sc until half way around work from first decrease, then *decrease one stitch*, mark the decrease just made, 1sc in each of remaining sc of round. 31sc.

Work one round without decreasing. Work 2 decreases evenly spaced on next round and on 2 following alternate rounds, working decreases as before and positioning them roughly above the marked decreases on the first decrease round. 25sc.

Continue in sc without shaping until work measures 12 1/2in/32cm. Decrease 2 stitches as before on next round and 3 following alternate rounds. 17sc.

Work in sc until work measures 17 3/4in/ 45cm.

Work a slip stitch in each of next few sc to taper the stitch height and neaten the edge. Fasten off.

TO FINISH

Weave the loose ends into the wrong side of the cover.

log
basket

For the ultimate in crochet, make a fireside basket in rich black leather, or sisal, string, or hemp and use it for logs, newspapers, magazines, or general clutter. Crocheting with leather thonging takes a little dexterity and patience, but the results are stunning. Worked in single crochet with a really large hook, the basket is made in five pieces that are then sewn together. Large "buttonholes" serve as handles. Work to dimensions that suit your budget and purpose.

BASKET SIZE

Approximately 15in x 12in x 10in
tall/37.5cm x 30cm x 25cm tall.

MATERIALS

9 x 55yd/50m balls 2mm-thick round
leather thronging (available from craft
stores or leather merchants); or sisal or
hemp string
Hook sizes K/10½ (7.00mm), L/11
(8.00mm), and N/13 (9.00mm)
Large upholstery sewing needle—optional

STITCH SIZE

This basket has a "gauge" (stitch size) of 8
stitches and 10 rows to 4in/10cm measured
over single crochet, but working to an exact
gauge is not essential (see Tips).

TECHNIQUES USED

Single crochet and joining in new balls
of yarn.

TIPS

Gauge and basket size

Don't worry about gauge too much!
As the basket can be made to any size, it
doesn't matter what your gauge is as long
as it produces a fairly stiff fabric that will
hold its shape nicely. Just make the sides
and ends of the basket following the
instructions given. Then make the base,
adding to or subtracting from the number
of rows recommended until the depth of
the piece matches the width of the ends.
If you wish to achieve a particular size, do
a small square to test your stitch size, then
calculate the number of rows and stitches
you'll need (see page 17).

Joining in a new yarn

This technique is used for starting a new
ball of yarn when the one you are using
runs out. Begin a single crochet in the
usual way, by drawing a loop through the
next stitch, then drop the old yarn and

draw the new yarn through both loops
now on the hook to finish the single
crochet (see Crochet Basics for how to
work single crochet). Leave a long loose
end of the old and new yarns to weave in
later, or work over the ends for several
stitches before clipping them off.

Leather

Leather is quite hard on the hands, so
concentrate on one stitch at a time, as
a unique aspect of constructing a special
textile. Warm the leather in your hands
as you work to soften it. It can be a little
sticky, too, and a little talcum powder on
the hook may assist to pull it through.

Sewing together

To sew the leather basket pieces
together, use a large upholstery needle.
Alternatively, you can simply weave the
end of the thronging directly through
the crochet fabric, as it is rigid enough
to do this.

INSPIRATION

Experiment with different yarn textures, sisal string or hemp. Make the basket in a texture of your choice and fill with supplies for a new home or baby, as a personal gift or to coordinate with the décor of a room.

METHOD

Basket sides (make 2)

Foundation chain Leaving a long loose end and using a size N/13 (9.00mm) hook and leather thonging, chain 30.

Change to a size L/11 (8.00mm) hook and begin working in single crochet as follows:

Row 1 Work 1sc into 2nd chain from hook, 1sc in each of remaining chains. Turn.

Row 2 Ch1 (this counts as first sc of row, so work it loosely), skip first sc and work 1sc in next sc, then work 1sc in each of remaining sc, work last sc in ch-1 at edge. Turn. There are 30 stitches in the row.

Repeat *row 2* until work measures 6 3/4in/17cm from foundation-chain edge—a total of about 17 rows from beginning.

"Buttonhole"/slot for handle

Start making the slot for the handle on the next row as follows:

Next row Ch1 (to count as first sc), skip first sc and work 1sc in next sc, then work 1sc in each of next 7sc. Turn. There are now 9 stitches in this short row.

Next row Ch1, skip first sc and work 1sc in next sc, then work 1sc in each of next 6sc, work last sc in ch-1 at edge. Turn. Leave the thonging where it is now—at the outside edge of the piece—but do not cut it off as you will return to it after working the other side of the slot.

Second side of slot

Using a new ball of thonging and with the piece facing you so that the short rows just worked are on the right, skip the first 12 stitches of the section left unworked and insert the hook into the next sc, yarn over hook and draw a loop through, ch1, skip next sc and work 1sc in next sc, 1sc in each of next 6sc, work last sc in ch-1 at edge. Turn. There are 9 stitches in this short row.

Next row Ch1, skip first sc and work 1sc in next sc, then work 1sc in each of next 6sc, work last sc in ch-1 at edge. Fasten off.

Join sides of slot

Return to first side of handle "buttonhole," pick up thonging left at outside edge and continue as follows:

Next row Ch1, skip first sc and work 1sc in next sc, then work 1sc in each of next 6sc, 1sc in ch-1 at handle edge, then chain 12 over the gap, 1sc in each of next 8sc on second side of handle, work last sc in ch-1 at edge. Turn.

Next row Ch1, skip first sc and work 1sc in next sc, 1sc in each of next 7sc, 1sc in each chain, 1sc in each of next 8sc, work last sc in ch-1 at edge. Turn. There are now 30 stitches in the row.

Now continue in sc until side measures 9 1/2in/24cm from foundation-chain edge—a total of about 24 rows from beginning. Fasten off.

Basket ends (make 2)

Foundation chain Leaving a long loose end and using a size N/13 (9.00mm) hook and leather thonging, chain 24.

Change to a size L/11 (8.00mm) hook and work *rows 1* and *2* as for basket sides.

Repeat *row 2* on these 24 stitches until there are same number of rows as on sides. Fasten off.

Basket base (make 1)

Foundation chain Leaving a long loose end and using a size N/13 (9.00mm) hook and leather thonging, chain 30.

Change to a size L/11 (8.00mm) hook and work *rows 1* and *2* as for basket sides.

Repeat *row 2* on these 30 stitches until work measures 12in/30cm from foundation-chain edge (check that it is deep enough to fit ends and adjust if necessary). Fasten off.

TO FINISH

Weave in all loose ends, taking care not to cut them off too short.

Join the ends and sides by overcast stitching with wrong sides together and pushing thronging through row ends or using a large upholstery needle (see Tips).

Attach base either by overcasting, or by working sc through both layers with a size K/10 1/2 (7.00mm) hook, so that the seam is on the outside.

Finally, to firm up the top edge of the basket, work a row of sc all around the top using a size K/10 1/2 (7.00mm) hook. Fasten off and weave in any remaining loose ends.

string bag

Made with colored plastic string, available in hardware or stationery stores, this string bag is very inexpensive to make and easy to work. Make several in different colors, filled with colorful plastic toys, to hang next to the nursery bathtub. Alternatively, hang them in the pantry, and fill them with fruit and vegetables. Work alternatives in natural twine or leather thonging, fill with seashells and driftwood, and hang them in the bathroom.

making : the string bag

BAG SIZE
Approximately 13in/33cm deep, but the bag is very stretchy.

MATERIALS
2 x 98yd/89m balls colored multipurpose polypropylene string (available from local hardware or stationery stores)
Hook size F/5 (4.00mm)
Length of contrasting colored yarn for marker

STITCH SIZE
This bag has a "gauge" (stitch size) of 5 chain-5 loops to 4in/10cm measured over crochet stitch used for bag, but working to an exact gauge is not essential (see Tips).

TECHNIQUES USED
Single crochet, working in rounds, working into chain spaces, and joining in new balls of yarn.

TIPS
Gauge
Don't worry about gauge too much! Because this is a string bag, you needn't work it to an exact size, and as it is worked round and round in a spiral, you can just keep working until the bag is the required size.

Working in rounds
When you work your crochet in rounds you never have to turn the fabric. The same side is always facing you.

Marking the beginning of a round
Be sure to mark the beginning of each round to make it easier to keep your place.

Joining in a new yarn
This technique is used for changing yarns when your ball of yarn is finished. Begin a single crochet in the usual way, by drawing a loop through the next stitch, then drop the old yarn and draw the new yarn through both loops now on the hook to finish the single crochet (see Crochet Basics). Leave a long loose end of the old yarn to weave in later.

METHOD
Foundation-chain ring Leaving a long loose end and using a size F/5 (4.00mm) hook, chain 4 and join length of chain into a ring by working a slip stitch into first chain made.

Round 1 Chain 1, work 8sc into ring, working over long loose end.

Before starting the next round, place a short length of a contrasting yarn across your crochet fabric from front to back, tight up against the loop on the hook and above the working yarn. Then start to work the single crochet of *round 2*, catching the marker in position. The marker will show you where the round started, as it will be caught under the top of the first stitch of the round.

inspiration

Take advantage of all the different types of string available and make several bags in different colors and textures. You could use cotton or linen knitting or crochet yarns as well—but make sure your bag is strong enough if you intend to carry heavy items in it.

Round 2 *Ch1, 1sc in next sc, repeat from * to end, making sure you are no longer working over loose end.

At the end of each round pull the marker out and place it across your crochet, up against the loop on the hook as before, so it will always be under the top of the first stitch of the round showing you where to start the next round.

Round 3 *Ch2, 1sc in next ch-1 space, repeat from * to end.

Round 4 *Ch3, 1sc in next ch-2 space, repeat from * to end. There are now 8 ch-3 spaces in the round.

Round 5 *[Ch3, 1sc] twice in next ch-3 space, repeat from * to end. 16 ch-3 spaces.

Rounds 6, 7, and 8 *Ch3, 1sc in next ch-3 space, repeat from * to end.

Round 9 *Ch5, 1sc in next ch-3 space, repeat from * to end.

Round 10 *[Ch5, 1sc] twice in next ch-5 space, ch5, 1sc in next ch-5 space, repeat from * to end. 24 ch-5 spaces.

Round 11 *Ch5, 1sc in next ch-5 space, repeat from * to end.

Rounds 12–14 Work 3 rounds as round 11.

Round 15 As round 10. 36 ch-5 spaces.

Rounds 16–21 Work 6 rounds as round 11.

Round 22 *Ch4, 1sc in next ch-5 space, repeat from * to end.

Round 23 *Ch3, 1sc in next ch-4 space, repeat from * to end.

Round 24 *Ch2, 1sc in next ch space, repeat from * to end.

Round 25 As round 24.

Round 26 *1sc in next sc, 2sc in next ch-2 space, repeat from * to end. 108sc.

Handles

Rounds 27 and 28 1sc in each of next 33sc, 52ch, skip next 21sc, 1sc in each of next 33sc, 52ch, skip next 21sc; now work

1sc in each sc and 1sc in each chain around top of bag and handles. Slip stitch in next sc and fasten off.

TO FINISH

Pull the long loose end at the center of the circle to tighten up the hole and weave it into the work. Weave in any other loose ends as well.

at home

turkish slippers

These stylish slippers were inspired by little Turkish shoes. They are worked in single crochet in a medium-weight, cotton yarn, used double, so they don't take long to make. Each slipper is worked in one piece, then the heel seam is joined at the back. For comfort, the sole is best lined with a ready-made insole. A simple felt lining in a toning color covers the insole.

making : the turkish slippers

SLIPPER SIZE

Approximately 9½(10½)in/24(27)cm
in length.
*The pattern is written for two women's sizes,
but is adjustable to suit your specific size.*

MATERIALS

4(4) x 1¾oz/50g balls Rowan *Handknit DK
Cotton* or a similar medium-weight yarn
(see page 122)
Hook sizes F/5 (4.00mm) and H/8 (5.00mm)
Length of contrasting yarn for marker
Large blunt-ended needle
Pair of ready-made insoles
Contrasting or toning colored felt to cover
top of insole
Fabric glue

STITCH SIZE

These slippers have a "gauge" (stitch size)
of 12½ stitches and 14 rows to 4in/10cm
measured over single crochet, using the
yarn double.

TECHNIQUES USED

Single crochet, working in rounds, simple
increases, and joining in new balls of yarn.

TIPS

Gauge

Make a swatch of single crochet to test
your stitch size. If you are getting more
than 12½ stitches to 4in/10cm, try a
larger hook size; less than 12½ stitches,
a smaller hook. Don't worry too much
about the number of rows to 4in/10cm
as you can easily adjust the length.

Working in rounds

When you work your crochet in rounds
you never have to turn the fabric. The right
side is always facing you.

Marking the beginning of a round

Be sure to mark the beginning of each
round to make it easier to keep your place.

Joining in a new yarn

This technique is used for changing yarns
when your ball of yarn is finished or when
you want to start a new color for stripes.
Begin a single crochet in the usual way, by
drawing a loop through the next stitch,
then drop the old yarn and draw the new
yarn through both loops now on the hook
to finish the single crochet. Leave a long
loose end of the old and new yarns to
weave in later, or work over the ends for
several stitches before clipping them off.

Joining the seam

Leave a long loose end when fastening off
the crochet after the last row of the
slipper. You can use this length for sewing
the back heel seam.

INSPIRATION

Experiment with different yarn textures,
heavier or finer yarns, or try regular-color
or random-color stripes. Instead of felt, use
a floral or stripe print to cover the insole,
or you may wish to edge the slipper
opening with a contrast or toning color
yarn or fabric.

METHOD

Foundation-chain ring Leaving a long loose end and using a size H/8 (5.00mm) hook and 2 strands of yarn together, chain 4 and join the length of chain into a ring by working a slip stitch into first chain made.

Round 1 (right side) Chain 1, work 6sc into ring, working over the long loose end; join with a slip stitch to top of first sc of round.

Round 2 (right side) Ch1, place a short length of a contrasting yarn across your crochet fabric from front to back, tight up against the loop on the hook and above the working yarn—called *place marker*—, 2sc in same place as slip stitch was worked, 2sc in each of remaining 5sc of round; join with a slip stitch to first sc of round (ignore slip stitch and ch-1 and work into top of first sc—your marker marks the spot). There are now 12sc in the round.

Round 3 Ch1, pull marker out of previous round and place marker as before, 1sc in same place as slip stitch, 1sc in each sc to end; join with a slip stitch to first sc. Continue to pull out your marker and place it after working the first chain of each round.

Round 4 Ch1, 1sc in same place as slip stitch, 2sc in the next sc, *1sc in next sc, 2sc in next sc, repeat from * to end; join with a slip stitch to first sc. 18sc.

Round 5 As round 3.

Round 6 Ch1, 1sc in same place as slip stitch, 1sc in each of next 4sc, 2sc in next sc, *1sc in each of next 5sc, 2sc in next sc, repeat from * to end; join with a slip stitch to first sc. 21sc.

Round 7 As round 3.

Round 8 Ch1, 1sc in same place as slip stitch, 1sc in each of next 5sc, 2sc in next sc, *1sc in each of next 6sc, 2sc in next sc, repeat from * to end; join with a slip stitch to first sc. 24sc.

Round 9 As round 3.

Round 10 Ch1, 1sc in same place as slip stitch, 1sc in each of next 6sc, 2sc in next sc, *1sc in each of next 7sc, 2sc in next sc, repeat from * to end; join with a slip stitch to first sc. 27sc.

Round 11 As round 3.

Round 12 Ch1, 1sc in same place as slip stitch, 1sc in each of next 7sc, 2sc in next sc, *1sc in each of next 8sc, 2sc in next sc, repeat from * to end; join with a slip stitch to first sc. 30sc.

Larger size only

Round 13 As round 3.

Round 14 Ch1, 1sc in same place as slip stitch, 1sc in each of next 8sc, 2sc in next sc, *1sc in each of next 9sc, 2sc in next sc, repeat from * to end; join with a slip stitch to first sc. 33sc.

Both sizes

Work without shaping (as *round 3*) until slipper measures 4¼(5½)in/11(14)cm— about 3(6) rounds.

Shape sole and sides

After joining with a slip stitch to first sc at end of last round as usual, work a slip stitch in each of the next 2sc. Turn the work.

Now work back and forth in rows for the rest of the slipper as follows:

Row 1 (wrong side) Ch1 (this chain counts as first sc of row, so work it loosely), 1sc in each of next 15sc. Turn.

Row 2 Ch1 (to count as first sc), skip first sc and work 1sc in next sc, 1sc in each of remaining sc, work last sc in ch-1 at edge. Turn. 16sc.

Work 2(4) rows more as *row 2*.

Next row (increase row) Ch1 (to count as first sc), 1sc in first sc, 1sc in each of remaining sc, 2sc in ch-1 at edge. Turn. 18sc.

Work 5 rows more as *row 2*, then repeat increase row once more. 20dc.

Continue in sc without increasing until work measures 9½(10½)in/24(27)cm or required foot length.

Fasten off (see Tips).

Work another slipper exactly the same.

TO FINISH

Pull the long loose end at the center of each toe to tighten up the hole and weave it into at the inside of the slipper. Weave in any other loose ends inside the slipper as well.

Steam and press the slippers lightly.

Fold the heel end of the slipper in half, with wrong sides together, and join the back heel seam.

Edging

Using a size F/5 (4.00mm) hook and one strand of yarn and with the right side of the slipper facing, begin at back seam and work 1 row of sc along the slipper opening on each slipper. For an even edging, work 1sc into each row end along the sides of the opening, and 1sc in each sc along the front of the opening. Fasten off and weave in end.

Insoles

Cut a two pieces of felt to the same size as the insoles and glue one piece to the top of each insole using fabric glue. Leave to dry, then insert insoles into slippers.

cafetière cover

No longer banished to the back of the kitchen drawer or cupboard, a tea cozy can take on a new guise—in this case as a sleek cover to keep the coffee warm at the breakfast table or in the office. This cafetière cover is worked in basic single crochet in a single color, but would look equally good in a stripe. The shapings are worked just inside the edge to produce a smooth and rounded shape. The little knob can be made in a contrasting color as an attractive finishing touch. To insulate the cover, line it with felt, which is widely available in most good craft stores.

making : the cafetière cover

COVER SIZE

Approximately 10in/25cm high x 8¾in/21.5cm wide (17½in/43cm in circumference). The cover is suitable for a small cafetière coffee pot.

MATERIALS

Plain cover

3 x 1¾oz/50g balls Rowan *Cotton Glacé* or a similar medium-weight mercerized cotton yarn (see page 122)

Hook size D/3 (3.00mm)

Piece of of colored felt for lining, 20in x 12in/50cm x 30cm

STITCH SIZE

This tea cozy has a "gauge" (stitch size) of 19 stitches and 23 rows to 4in/10cm measured over single crochet, but working to an exact gauge is not essential (see Tips).

TECHNIQUES USED

Single crochet, simple decreases, joining in new balls of yarn, and working in rounds.

TIPS

Gauge

Don't worry about gauge too much! Because this is a cafetière cozy, working to an exact size is not that important as long as the cozy will slip easily over your coffee pot.

Working in rounds

When you work your crochet in rounds you never have to turn the fabric. The right side is always facing you.

Marking the beginning of a round

Be sure to mark the beginning of each round to make it easier to keep your place.

Joining in a new yarn

This technique is used for changing yarns when your ball of yarn is finished or when you want to start a new color for stripes. Change to a new yarn at the end of a row. Begin the last single crochet of the row in the usual way, by drawing a loop through the last stitch, then drop the old yarn and draw the new yarn through both loops now on the hook to finish the single crochet (see Crochet Basics).

Leave a long loose end of the old and new yarns to weave in later, or work over the ends for several stitches before clipping them off.

METHOD

Front

Foundation chain Leaving a long loose end and using a size D/3 (3.00mm) hook, chain 42.

Row 1 Work 1sc into 3rd chain from hook, 1sc in each of remaining chains. Turn.

Row 2 Ch1 (this counts as first sc of row, so work it loosely), skip first sc and work 1sc in next sc, then work 1sc in each of remaining sc, work last sc in ch at edge. Turn. There are 41 stitches in the row.

Repeat *row 2* until work measures 6¾in/ 17cm from foundation-chain edge—a total of about 39 rows from beginning.

Top shaping

Begin shaping the top by decreasing one stitch at each end of the next row as follows:

Next row (decrease row) Ch1 to count as first sc, skip first sc, 1sc in next sc, [insert hook in next sc, yarn over hook and draw a loop through] twice, yarn over hook and draw through all 3 loops on hook—called *decrease one stitch*—, work 1sc in each sc to last 4 stitches, then decrease one stitch by working next 2sc together as before, 1sc in each of last 2 stitches. Turn. 39sc.

Work one row without decreases (as *row 2*). **Repeat the decrease row.

Work one row without decreases.** 37sc. Repeat from ** to ** once more. 35sc. Repeat the decrease row 12 times. 11sc. Fasten off.

Back

Make another piece the same for the back of the cover.

TO FINISH

Weave in any loose ends at the back of the work. Lay the pieces out flat, then steam and press lightly.

Lining

Using one piece of the cozy as a template, cut out two pieces of felt to the same size and shape, but allowing an extra 5/8in/ 1.5cm all around the curved edge for the seam allowance.

Place the crochet pieces together with the right sides facing each other, line up the stitches, and pin. Then sew the pieces together and turn right side out.

Next, sew the lining pieces together and trim the seam. Place the lining inside the cozy, trim the bottom edge if necessary and stitch to the bottom edge of the cozy.

Bobble

For a detail that can be used to pull off the cover, make a little bobble as follows:

Foundation chain Leaving a long loose end and using a size D/3 (3.00mm) hook, chain 2.

Round 1 (right side) Work 6sc into 2nd chain from hook; join with a slip stitch to top of first sc of round.

Round 2 (right side) Ch1, place a short length of a contrasting yarn across your crochet fabric from front to back, tight up against the loop on the hook and above the working yarn—called *place marker*—, 2sc in same place as slip stitch was worked, 2sc in each of remaining 5sc of round; join with a slip stitch to first sc of round (ignore slip stitch and ch-1 and work into top of first sc—your marker marks the spot). There are now 12sc in the round.

Round 3 Ch1, pull marker out of previous round and place marker as before, 1sc in same place as slip stitch, 1sc in each sc to end; join with a slip stitch to first sc. Continue to pull out your marker and place it at the beginning of each round.

Round 4 Ch1, 1sc in same place as slip stitch, 2sc in the next sc, *1sc in next sc, 2sc in next sc, repeat from * to end; join with a slip stitch to first sc. 18sc.

Round 5 As round 3.

Round 6 Ch1, 1sc in same place as slip stitch, *skip next sc, 1sc in next sc, repeat from * to last sc, skip last sc; join with a slip stitch to first sc. 9sc.

Stuff bobble with small amount of matching yarn to pad it.

Round 7 Ch1, 1sc in same place as slip stitch, *skip next sc, 1sc in next sc, repeat from * to end. 5sc.

Fasten off leaving a long length of yarn. Use the long end to sew the opening closed, then stitch to the top of the cover.

inspiration

Experiment with different yarn textures, stitch patterns, or colors for your coffee-pot cozy. Or try contrasting plain or patterned linings. As accessories for your cafetière cover, make little crochet coasters for your coffee mugs using up leftover yarn. Work squares in the stitch of your choice and add white stripes to the basic black theme. Edge the squares with a round of single crochet to finish them off.

towel edging

Crochet edgings add a touch of femininity to plain towels or bed linen. This simple, easy-to-make edging can either be crocheted as a separate strip and slip-stitched onto a towel, or worked directly into the hem of the towel. Although the towel and edging here are both in natural, crisp white cotton, you can work the crochet edging in any color and weight of yarn you like.

making : the towel edging

EDGING SIZE

The edging is approximately 1¼in/3cm deep and can be made to fit any size towel—the towel pictured is 26in/66cm wide (see Tips).

MATERIALS

1 x 1oz/25g ball of fine cotton yarn (enough for two strips of edging 26in/ 66cm long)
Hook size 6 steel (1.75mm)
Cotton towel of your choice (or alternative item to trim)

STITCH SIZE

This edging has a "gauge" (stitch size) of 24 stitches (6 scallops) to 4in/10cm

measured over edging pattern, but working to an exact gauge is not essential (see Tips for more information).

TECHNIQUES USED

Single crochet, double crochet, working into a chain loop, and making picots.

TIPS

Gauge and edging measurements
Don't worry about gauge too much! The size of your edging will depend on the thickness of the yarn, and if your yarn is slightly thinner or thicker than the one used here, your gauge may not match the one given above. Test your gauge before starting the edging. Chain 34 and work

the edging pattern from *row 1*. If your stitch size is different than the one recommended, then use your swatch to determine how many scallops you'll need to fit your towel.

Working into a chain loop
When working the last row of the scallop edging, work the single crochet into the chain loop by inserting hook *under* the chain—not *into* it. This covers the chain completely and gives the scallop a "bound" look for an ornate edge.

Crocheting into the towel edge
If the weave of your towel is loose enough and your hook fine enough to pierce the towel, you can work your edging directly onto the towel. Work a

Try working your crochet lace edgings with linen or silk threads for a touch of luxury and contrast. Play with using colored yarns as well. Then think of alternative projects to trim, such as pillowcases, pillows, sheets and duvet covers. Even curtains can be given a bohemian vintage look. For quick-to-make edgings, experiment with thicker yarns, and for delicate items, use finer threads.

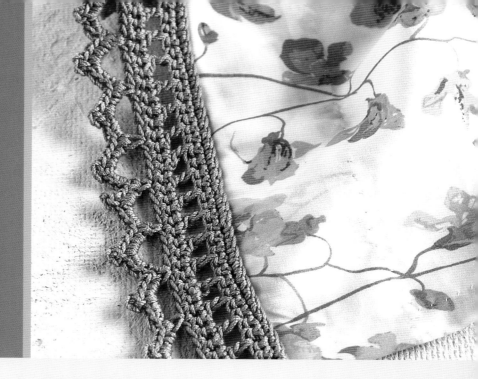

multiple of 4 single crochets, plus 1 single crochet extra, evenly along the edge—this will give one scallop for every 4sc worked. Then turn the work and start following the edging pattern from *row 2*.

METHOD

Foundation chain Determine how many scallops you need (see Tips); then leaving a long loose end and using a size 6 steel (1.75mm) hook, make a multiple of 4 chains (4 chains for each scallop) plus 2 extra. (For the 26in/66cm wide towel shown, 39 scallops were worked onto a foundation chain of 158 chains.)

Row 1 Work 1sc into 2nd chain from hook, 1sc in each of remaining chains. Turn.

Row 2 Ch1, 1sc in each sc to end. Turn.

Row 3 Ch4 to count as first dc and first ch-1 space, skip first 2sc, 1dc in next sc, *ch1, skip next sc, 1dc in next sc, repeat from * to end. Turn.

Row 4 Ch1, 1sc in first dc, *1sc in next ch-1 space (inserting hook *under* the chain—not *into* the chain—when working the sc), 1sc in next dc, repeat from * to turning chain at end of row, 1sc in turning-chain space, 1sc in 2nd chain from last dc. Turn.

Row 5 Ch1, 1sc in each sc to end. Turn.

Row 6 Ch1, 1sc in first sc, *6ch, skip next 3sc, 1sc in next sc, repeat from * to end. Turn.

Row 7 (picot row) Ch1, 1sc in first

sc, [3sc, ch3 (for picot), 3sc] all in each ch-6 loop to end (see Tips), 1sc in last sc. Fasten off.

This completes the edging.

Work another piece in the same way for the other end of the towel.

TO FINISH

Weave in any loose ends. Steam edging gently to flatten. Pin the edgings to the ends of the towel, slightly stretching or easing in if necessary, and overcast stitch securely in place.

raffia table mats

Made in a simple crochet cluster pattern with richly colored green raffia,

these rectangular mats are ideal for informal meals or for eating al fresco.

They are one of the easiest projects in this book to make—one mat should

take you no longer than a few hours at most. As the pattern is so basic,

you could make them on the bus or train.

making : the raffia table mats

TABLE MAT SIZE

Approximately 18in x 13³⁄4in/46cm x 35cm (see Tips).

MATERIALS

Raffia for a set of four table mats (buy one ball from a craft or stationery stores and test it to see how far it will go) Hooks size F/5 (4.00mm) and H/8 (5.00mm)

STITCH SIZE

These mats have a "gauge" (stitch size) of approximately 8 clusters and 8 cluster rows to 4in/10cm measured over the cluster stitch pattern, but working to an exact gauge is not essential (see Tips.)

TECHNIQUES USED

Simple double-crochet clusters, single crochet edging, and joining in new balls of raffia.

TIPS

Working the foundation chain
Be sure to use a larger hook for the foundation chain, so that the starting edge is not too tight. This will help the mat lay flat.

Gauge
Achieving an exact gauge is not essential, as you can easily alter the number of clusters and rows you work (see Inspiration box at the top of the opposite page for how to do this).

Joining in a new ball
This technique is used for joining in a new ball of raffia when your old one runs out or for changing colors when working stripes. Work your cluster in the usual way, but change to the new ball of yarn when drawing through the last loop that joins the 3-dc group at the top. Leave a long loose end of the old raffia and the new raffia to weave in later.

METHOD

Foundation chain Leaving a long loose end and using a size H/8 (5.00mm) hook, chain 74.

Change to a size F/5 (4.00mm) hook and begin the cluster stitch pattern as follows:

Row 1 [Wrap yarn over hook and insert hook through 4th chain from hook, yarn over hook and draw a loop through, yarn over hook and draw through first 2 loops on hook] twice (working each st into the same chain), yarn over hook and draw through all 3 loops on hook—this completes the *beginning cluster*—, *ch1, skip 1ch, [yarn over hook and insert hook into next ch, yarn over hook and draw a loop through, yarn over hook and draw through first 2 loops on hook] 3 times (working each st into the same chain), yarn over hook and draw through all 4 loops on hook—this completes the *cluster*—, repeat from * to end of

inspiration

You may wish to make your mats a different size—this is very easy to do. For example, for a 5in/13cm square coaster, start with 20 foundation chains, then work *row 1* of the table mat pattern. This will give you 9 clusters across the row. Continue until you have completed 9 rows of the cluster pattern and fasten off. Then work the single-crochet edging as for the table mat. Work other sizes in the same way, starting with a foundation chain that has 4 chains for the first cluster and 2 chains for every extra cluster.

foundation chain. Turn. There are 36 clusters across the row.

Row 2 Ch3 to count as first st in beginning cluster, [wrap yarn over hook and insert hook through top of first cluster in previous row, yarn over hook and draw a loop through, yarn over hook and draw through first 2 loops on hook] twice (working each st into the top of the same cluster), yarn over hook and draw through all 3 loops on hook—this completes the *beginning cluster*—, *ch1, [yarn over hook and insert hook through top of next cluster, yarn over hook and draw a loop through, yarn over hook and draw through first 2 loops on hook] 3 times (working each st into the top of the same cluster stitch), yarn over hook and draw through all 4 loops on hook—this completes the *cluster*—, repeat from * to end of row. Turn.

Repeat *row 2* until the mat measures

about 13¼in/34cm from the foundation-chain edge (a total of about 27 rows from beginning). Fasten off.

Make three more mats in the same way to complete the set.

TO FINISH

Weave in any loose ends at the back of each mat.

If it is necessary to flatten it, lay the table mat out flat and leave overnight under a pile of books.

Edging

Using a size F/5 (4.00mm) hook, work a row of single crochet around the edge of each mat. Both sides of the mats are the same—which means there is no right side or wrong side—so you can work the edging with either side facing you.

For an even edging, work 1sc in each chain along the foundation chain edge; 1sc in each ch and 1sc in each cluster along the

top of the last row; 2sc into each row end along the short sides; and 3sc into each corner to keep the mat square. Fasten off and weave in end.

tea cozy

Retro-style crochet is back, reinvented. This little teapot cover is a timeless classic. Worked in single crochet in bright random stripes of color in mercerized cotton, it is lined with contrasting gingham fabric and insulated with batting. A little, curled, crocheted stem at the top adds a finishing touch, doubling up as useful handle.

making : the tea cozy

COZY SIZE

Approximately 8³/₄in/22cm high x
12⁵/₈in/31.5cm wide (25¹/₄in/63cm in
circumference). The cozy is suitable for
a small teapot.

MATERIALS

Rowan *Cotton Glacé* or a similar
medium-weight mercerized cotton yarn
(see page 122) in 8 contrasting colors
as follows:
Color A: 1 x 1³/₄oz/50g ball in purple
Color B: 1 x 1³/₄oz/50g ball in black
Color C: 1 x 1³/₄oz/50g ball in white
Color D: 1 x 1³/₄oz/50g ball in turquoise
Color E: 1 x 1³/₄oz/50g ball in light sage
Color F: 1 x 1³/₄oz/50g ball in dark sage
Color G: 1 x 1³/₄oz/50g ball in pink
Color H: 1 x 1³/₄oz/50g ball in orange
Hook size D/3 (3.00mm)
Piece of batting to insulate cozy

12in/30cm of 44in/112cm wide black and
white gingham fabric for lining

STITCH SIZE

This tea cozy has a "gauge" (stitch size) of
19 stitches and 23 rows to 4in/10cm
measured over single crochet, but working
to an exact gauge is not essential (see Tips).

TECHNIQUES USED

Single crochet, simple decreases, and
joining in new balls of yarn.

TIPS
Gauge
Don't worry about gauge too much!
Because this is a tea cozy, working to an
exact size is not that important as long as
the cozy will slip easily over your teapot.
Joining in a new yarn
This technique is used for changing yarns

when your ball of yarn is finished or when
you want to start a new color for stripes.
Change to a new yarn at the end of a row
on the tea cozy. Begin the last single
crochet of the row in the usual way, by
drawing a loop through the last sc, then
drop the old yarn and draw the new yarn
through both loops now on the hook to
finish the single crochet (see Crochet
Basics). Leave a long loose end of the old
and new yarns to weave in later, or work
over the ends for several stitches before
clipping them off.

INSPIRATION

Experiment with different yarn textures
and/or different color combinations for
your tea cozy. For a homemade touch,
work your tea cozy in random black and
white cotton stripes and line with bold
black and white ticking.

METHOD

Front

Foundation chain Leaving a long loose end and using a size D/3 (3.00mm) hook and color A (purple), chain 61.

Row 1 Using color A (purple), work 1sc into 2nd chain from hook, 1sc in each of remaining chains, dropping A and drawing through B (black) when completing last loop of last sc of row (see Tips). Turn. There are 60 stitches in the row.

Row 2 Using color B (black), ch1, 1sc in each sc to end of row. Turn.

Continuing to repeat *row 2* to form the single crochet fabric and changing colors with the last loop of the row before, work in stripes as follows:

Color B (black): 1 row.
Color C (white): 1 row.
Color B (black): 1 row.
Color D (turquoise): 3 rows.
Color E (light sage): 1 row.
Color F (dark sage): 2 rows.
Color G (pink): 5 rows.
Color H (orange): 2 rows.
Color B (black): 2 rows.
Color E (light sage): 1 row.
Color B (black): 1 row.
Color E (light sage): 2 rows.
Color D (turquoise): 1 row.

Top shaping

Using color D (turquoise), begin shaping the top by decreasing one stitch at each end of the next row as follows:

Next row (decrease row) Insert hook into first sc, yarn over hook and draw a loop through, insert hook into next sc, yarn over hook and draw a loop through, yarn over hook and draw through all 3 loops on hook—called *decrease one stitch*—, work 1sc each sc to last 2sc, then decrease one

stitch by working last 2sc together as before. Turn. 58sc.

Repeating the decrease row when instructed, continue working single crochet in stripes as follows:

Using color C (white), work one row without shaping (as *row 2*).

[Using color F (dark sage), repeat decrease row, then work one row without shaping] twice. 54sc.

Still using color F (dark sage), repeat decrease row. 52sc.

Using color E (light sage), work one row without shaping, then repeat decrease row. 50sc.

Using color A (purple), repeat decrease row. 48sc.

Using color C (white), repeat decrease row. 46sc.

Using color H (orange), work one row without shaping.

Using color B (black), repeat decrease row, then work one row without shaping. 44sc.

Using color A (purple), repeat decrease row twice. 40sc.

Using color G (pink), repeat decrease row twice, then work one row without shaping. 36sc.

Using color C (white), repeat decrease row. 34sc.

Using color B (black), repeat decrease row twice. 30sc.

Using color E (light sage), repeat decrease row twice, then work one row without shaping. 26sc.

Still using color E (light sage), slip stitch to last 2sc.

Fasten off.

Back

Make another piece the same for the back of the tea cozy.

TO FINISH

Weave in any loose ends at the back of the work.

Lay the pieces out flat, then steam and press lightly.

Lining

Using one piece of the cozy as a template, cut out two pieces of lining fabric to the same size and shape, but allowing an extra 5/8in/1.5cm all around each piece for the seam allowance. Cut two pieces of batting the same shape and size as the lining pieces.

Place the crochet pieces together with the right sides facing each other, line up the stitches, and pin. Then sew the pieces together and turn right side out.

Place the fabric lining pieces together with the right sides facing each other and sew together along the curved edge. Sew the batting pieces together in the same way and trim the seams.

Place the batting inside the crocheted tea cozy and trim the bottom edge to the same length as the tea cozy. Then place the lining inside. Turn up the hem of the lining all around the bottom edge and join to the cozy edge with small, neat stitches.

Stem

For a functional detail that can be used to pull off the tea cozy, make a little stalk as follows:

Using the color of your choice and a size D/3 (3.00mm) hook, chain 10.

Work 6 rows of single crochet and fasten off.

Allowing the crochet to roll in on itself, sew the foundation-chain edge to the last row to form a curled tube shape.

Stitch the stem securely to the top of the cozy.

runner

For informal meals with friends, eating al fresco, or for relaxed parties, set out a runner on the floor, or on a long low table, with platters of food. This simple runner is worked in twine in single crochet with borders of colored linen yarn—a modern variation on a traditional piece. If you prefer, work the borders in bright contrasting colors.

The stylish strip border on the runner forms interesting details at the corners. But if you're in a hurry, you can add a simpler border by working single crochet round and round the twine rectangle, mitering the corners as you go. For an even edging, work 1sc in each stitch or row end and 3sc at each corner for the miter. Add stripes, or work just the final row in a contrasting color for a smart finishing detail.

making : the runner

RUNNER SIZE

Approximately 16in x 58¹/₂in/40cm x 146cm.

MATERIALS

7 x 93yd/85m balls thick kitchen twine (available from local hardware or stationery stores)

Rowan *Linen Drape* or a similar lightweight linen yarn (see page 122) in 4 contrasting colors as follows:

Color A: 2 x 1³/₄oz/50g balls in yellow
Color B: 2 x 1³/₄oz/50g balls in charcoal
Color C: 1 x 1³/₄oz/50g balls in olive
Color D: 1 x 1³/₄oz/50g balls in pale olive
Hook sizes H/8 (5.00mm) and J/10 (6.00mm)

STITCH SIZE

This runner has a "gauge" (stitch size) of 11 stitches and 14 rows to 4in/10cm measured over single crochet and using a single strand of twine or two strands of lightweight yarn—but working to an exact gauge is not essential (see Tips).

TECHNIQUES USED

Single crochet, simple borders, and joining in new balls of yarn.

TIPS

Working the foundation chain

Be sure to use a larger hook for the foundation row, so that the starting edge is not too tight. This will help the runner to lay flat.

Gauge and runner size

Don't worry about gauge too much! Because this is a runner, an exact size is not that important as long as it suits your table. You can make the runner to any length you want by adding to or subtracting from the number of foundation chains, and to any width by working more or fewer rows.

Using yarn double

The colored linen yarns are used double throughout. If the color only calls for one ball of yarn, wind the ball off into two balls so it is ready to use double.

Joining in a new yarn

This technique is used for starting a new ball of yarn. Begin a single crochet in the usual way, by drawing a loop through the next stitch, then drop the old yarn and draw the new yarn through both loops now on the hook to finish the single crochet. Leave a long loose end of the old and new yarns to weave in later, or work over the ends for several stitches before clipping them off.

Joining on new colors for borders
When joining on a new color for the borders, insert the hook through the first stitch and draw a loop through, then continue as usual in single crochet, repeating *row 2* of the pattern.

METHOD

Foundation chain Leaving a long loose end and using a size J/10 (6.00mm) hook and twine, chain 154.

Change to a size H/8 (5.00mm) hook and begin working in single crochet as follows:

Row 1 Work 1sc into 2nd chain from hook, 1sc in each of remaining chains. Turn.

Row 2 Ch1 (this counts as first sc of row, so work it loosely), skip first sc and work 1sc in next sc, then work 1sc in each of remaining sc, work last sc in ch-1 at edge. Turn. There are 154 stitches in the row.

Repeat *row 2* until work measures 13½in/34cm from foundation-chain edge—a total of about 46 rows from beginning. Fasten off.

Borders
Using a size H/8 (5.00mm) hook and color A (yellow) double, join yarn to last row worked and work 6 rows in single crochet along this edge. (See Tips for joining on new colors for borders.)
Fasten off.

Using a size H/8 (5.00mm) hook and color B (charcoal) double, join yarn to foundation-chain edge and work 6 rows in single crochet along this edge. Fasten off.

Using a size H/8 (5.00mm) hook and color C (olive) double, join yarn to one short end and work 6 rows in single crochet along this edge. (For an even border, work 1sc into each row end.) Fasten off.

Work 6 rows in single crochet along the other short end in the same way, but using color D (pale olive).

TO FINISH

Weave any loose ends into the single crochet.

Lay the work out flat, then steam and press lightly.

useful information

helpful hints for beginners

The section on Crochet Basics on pages 14–27 shows you how to work the basic stitches in crochet. The following information may be helpful to you when creating crochet projects, either from this book or any other patterns you find.

You can choose to use the recommended yarns, or you can substitute others (see page 122 for information on yarn weights and types so you can choose suitable alternatives). Whether you choose to use the recommended yarns, or ones of your own choice, you must check that you are working to the appropriate gauge, or the item you are making may turn out a very different size! See pages 16 and 17 for information on checking gauge. Having said that, if you are making a throw, for example, and do not mind too much if it is a little bigger or smaller than the one shown in the pattern, then do not worry too much about stitch size. This is true of pillows, too, unless you wish to create a cover to fit a specific-size pillow form, when, of course, the gauge and the finished size will be important.

Certain yarns are easier to crochet with than others; those that are pliable and soft on the hands are the best for beginners, so select projects with soft cotton yarns to start with. Crocheting with string (or twine) is not difficult, but as it is less pliable than cotton it takes a little more dexterity initially, as indeed does leather, which benefits from being warmed before use.

PATTERN INFORMATION

The instructions for crochet projects are usually given in writing. The basic abbreviations used in pattern writing are shown opposite, although these can vary, so always check the abbreviations guide in any crochet book first. One area of potential confusion is that U.K. terminology is different than U.S. terminology. In the U.K., single crochet is called double crochet, for example, while double crochet is known as treble crochet, and so on.

In some instances in crochet it is easier to present the pattern information in charted form. This is particularly true of filet crochet where the pattern forms a grid, and can be most easily understood from a chart drawn on graph paper. Each "block" or "space" is represented by one square of the graph.

Most patterns have elements that repeat. There is an asterisk at the beginning of the repeat element of the pattern, or it is placed inside two asterisks or brackets. The number of times this sequence is repeated is indicated outside the asterisks or brackets, along with any additional stitches required to complete a row.

PRACTICE MAKES PERFECT

You will find that the speed and ease with which you crochet is simply a matter of practice. It is a good idea to test your skills on very simple stitches, possibly making a few gauge swatches first. (You can always stitch them together later to make a patchwork pillow!)

ABBREVIATIONS

To make the instructions for the crochet patterns easier to follow for beginners, very few abbreviations have been used in the book. However, the following lists cover the main abbreviations you may come across in other crochet patterns as well:

abbreviations for crochet stitches

ch	chain
dc	double crochet
dtr	double treble
hdc	half double
sc	single crochet
sl st	slip stitch
tr	treble
trtr	triple treble

other abbreviations

alt	alternate
approx	approximately
beg	begin(ning)
cm	centimeter(s)
cont	continu(e)(ing)
dec	decreas(e)(ing)
foll	follow(s)(ing)
g	gram(s)
in	inch(es)
inc	increas(e)(ing)
m	meter(s)
mm	millimeter(s)
oz	ounce(s)
pat(s)	pattern(s)

rem	remain(s)(ing)
rep	repeat(s)(ing)
RS	right side
st(s)	stitch(es)
tog	together
WS	wrong side
yd	yard(s)
yo	yarn over (hook)
*	Repeat instructions after an asterisk or between asterisks as many times as instructed.
[]	Repeat instructions inside brackets as many times as instructed.

CROCHET HOOKS

Here is a conversion chart for the various systems of hook sizes—just in case you have old hooks you'd like to use but aren't sure what they are equivalent to.

hook conversion chart

Metric	U.S.	old U.K.
.60mm	14 steel	
.75mm	12 steel	
1.00mm	11 steel	
1.50mm	8 steel	
1.75mm	6 steel	
2.00mm	B/1	14
2.50mm	C/2	12
3.00mm	D/3	10
3.50mm	E/4	9
4.00mm	F/5	8
4.50mm	G/6	7
5.00mm	H/8	6
5.50mm	I/9	5
6.00mm	J/10	4
6.50mm		3
7.00mm	K/10$\frac{1}{2}$	2
8.00mm	L/11	
9.00mm	N/13	
10.00mm	P/15	
16.00mm	Q	

If you have taken the time and trouble to create your own crochet textiles, you will want to make sure that they remain in good condition. The great variety of yarns on the market has necessitated some kind of international labeling standards for their care, which is usually indicated on the yarn label. While some yarns can be successfully dry cleaned (check the symbols on the yarn labels), many more are better washed carefully by hand. A few can be machine washed at appropriate temperatures. Again, all this information should be on the yarn label.

GENERAL HAND WASHING GUIDELINES

- If the article requires hand washing, then make sure that you use gentle soap flakes which must be dissolved before emersing it. Do not use very hot water to wash any wool yarn. Hand-hot temperatures are best.

- Always rinse the article at least twice in tepid water.

- Don't wring it roughly by hand; it is best to give it a short spin in the machine or, with delicate yarns, to wrap it in a towel and squeeze out the moisture gently.

- Pull the article gently into shape and hang it over a towel to dry, preferable on a flat surface.

MACHINE WASHING GUIDELINES

The temperature guidelines found on machines are as follows:

140°F/60°C hot: Hotter than the hand can bear; the temperature of most domestic hot water
120°F/50°C hand hot: As hot as the hand can stand
104°F/40°C warm: Just warm to the touch
86°F/30°C cool: Cool to the touch

CARE OF SPECIAL YARNS

- Mercerized cotton, soft cotton, and fine cotton are best washed by hand. Rinse well. Squeeze gently in a towel to remove surplus moisture and hang flat to dry.

- Heavy-weight cottons can be washed in a machine on a cool wash; check the yarn label. Short spin only. Dry flat.

- Lurex, mohair, and chenille are best dry cleaned in certain solvents. Check with your dry cleaner. Air well after cleaning.

- String, leather, sisal, hemp, and raffia cannot normally be dry cleaned and are best sponged down with a damp cloth and left to dry naturally.

s u b s t i t u t i n g   y a r n s

Although I have recommended a specific Rowan yarn for many of the projects in the book, you can substitute others. A description of each of the yarns used is given below.

If you decide to use an alternative yarn, any other make of yarn that is of the same weight and type should serve as well, but to avoid disappointing results, it is very important that you test the yarn first. Purchase a substitute yarn that is as close as possible to the original in thickness, weight, and texture so that it will be compatible with the crochet instructions. Buy only one ball to start with, so you can try out the effect. Calculate the number of balls you will need by yardage/meterage rather than by weight. The recommended knitting-needle size and knitting gauge on the ball bands are extra guides to the yarn thickness.

ROWAN YARNS

Rowan All Seasons Cotton
A medium-weight (aran-weight) cotton yarn with a soft, lofty texture
Recommended knitting-needle size: U.S. sizes 7–9/4^{1}/2–5^{1}/2mm
Gauge: 16–18 stitches x 23–25 rows per 4in/10cm over knitted stockinette stitch
Ball size: 99yd/90m per 1^{3}/4oz/50g ball
Yarn specification: cotton blend; 24 shades

Rowan Cotton Glacé
A medium-weight (between the double knitting and 4 ply) mercerized cotton yarn
Recommended knitting-needle size: U.S. sizes 3–5/3–3^{1}/4mm
Gauge: 23 stitches x 32 rows per 4in/10cm over knitted stockinette stitch
Ball size: 137yd/115m per 1^{3}/4oz/50g ball
Yarn specification: 100% cotton; 24 shades

Rowan 4ply Cotton
A lightweight (4-ply) cotton yarn
Recommended knitting-needle size: U.S. sizes 2–3/3mm
Gauge: 27–29 stitches x 37–39 rows per 4in/10cm over knitted stockinette stitch
Ball size: 186yd/170m per 1^{3}/4oz/50g ball
Yarn specification: 100% cotton; 18 shades

Rowan Handknit DK Cotton
A medium-weight (double-knitting-weight) yarn
Recommended knitting-needle size: U.S. sizes 6–7/4–4^{1}/2mm
Gauge: 19–20 stitches x 28 rows per 4in/10cm over knitted stockinette stitch
Ball size: 93yd/85m per 1^{3}/4oz/50g ball
Yarn specification: 100% cotton; 25 shades

Rowan Linen Drape
A lightweight linen yarn
Recommended knitting-needle size: U.S. sizes 3–6/3^{1}/4–4mm
Gauge: 22–24 stitches x 28–30 rows per 4in/10cm over knitted stockinette stitch
Ball size: 110yd/100m per 1^{3}/4oz/50g ball
Yarn specification: linen blend; 14 shades

Rowan Lurex Shimmer
A fine metallic yarn
Recommended knitting-needle size: U.S. size 3/3^{1}/4mm
Gauge: 29 stitches x 41 rows per 4in/10cm over knitted stockinette stitch
Ball size: 104yd/95m per 1oz/25g ball
Yarn specification: viscose blend; 6 shades

OTHER YARNS

Fine cotton threads specially designed for crochet lace are widely available in craft stores. The cotton thread used for the lace edging on pages 102–105 was obtained from: Yeoman Yarns Ltd., 36 Churchill Way, Fleckney, Leicester, LE8 8UD, U.K. Tel: 0116 2404464.

Leather thonging is available in craft stores or from leather merchants/saddlery shops. The 2mm-thick round leather thonging used for the basket on pages 84–87 and the floor pillow on pages 38–41 was obtained from: J.T. Batchelor Ltd., Leather Merchants, 9–10 Culford Mews, London N1 4DZ, U.K. Tel: 020 7254 2962.

String (or twine) comes in various thicknesses and is not always labeled with an exact amount, so you may need to experiment with a single ball to start with. The round pillow (pages 30–33), the boxes (pages 76–79), the bottle cover (pages 80–83), and the runner (pages 114–117) were made with natural-colored kitchen twine, which is available from hardware and stationery stores.

The colored polypropylene string used for the string bag on pages 88–91 is available from do-it-yourself and stationery stores.

yarn suppliers

SELECTED ROWAN STOCKISTS

See previous page for information about the Rowan yarns used in this book. To obtain Rowan yarns, look below to find a distributor or store in your area. For more information, contact Rowan head office in England or the Rowan website.

Website: **www.knitrowan.com**
Rowan, Green Lane Mill, Holmfirth, West Yorkshire HD9 2DX, England. Telephone: + 44 (0) 1484 681 881. Fax: + 44 (0) 1484 687 920.

ROWAN STOCKISTS IN U.S.A.
AGENT: Rowan USA, 4 Townsend West, Suite 8, Nashua, NH 03064. Tel: (603) 886-5041/5043. E-mail: wfibers@aol.com

ALABAMA
HUNTSVILLE: Yarn Expressions, 7914 S Memorial Parkway, AL 35802. Tel: (256) 881-0260. Website: www.yarnexpressions.com

ARIZONA
TUCSON: Purls, 7862 North Oracle Road, AZ 85704. Tel: (520) 797-8118.

ARKANSAS
LITTLE ROCK: The Handworks Gallery, 2911 Kavanaugh, AR 72205. Tel: (501) 664-6300. Website: www.handworksgallery.com

CALIFORNIA
ANAHEIM HILLS: Velona Needlecraft, 5701 M Santa Ana Canyon Road, Anaheim Hills, CA 92807. Tel: (714) 974-1570. Website: www.velona.com
CARMEL: Knitting by the Sea, 5th & Junipero, Carmel, CA 93921. Tel: (800) 823 3189.
BERKELEY: eKnitting.com, 1625 University Ave., Berkeley, CA 94703. Tel: (800) 392-6494. Website: eKnitting.com

LA JOLLA: Knitting in La Jolla, 7863 Girard Avenue, La Jolla, CA 92037. Tel: (800) 956-5648.
LONG BEACH: Alamitos Bay Yarn Co., 174 Marina Dr., Long Beach, CA 90803. Tel: (562) 799-8484. Website: www.yarncompany.com
LAFAYETTE: Big Sky Studio, 961 - C Moraga Rd., Lafayette, CA 94549. Tel: (925) 284 1020. Website: www.bigskystudio.com
LOS ALTOS: Uncommon Threads, 293 State St., Los Altos, CA 94022. Tel: (650) 941-1815.
MENDICINO: Mendicino Yarn, 45066 Ukiah Street, Mendicino, CA 95460. Tel: (888) 530-1400. Website: www.mendicinoyarnshop.com
OAKLAND: The Knitting Basket, 2054 Mountain Boulevard, Oakland, CA 94611. Tel: (800) 654-4887.
Website: theknittingbasket.com
REDONDO BEACH: L'Atelier, 17141/2 Catalina, Redondo Beach, CA 90277. Tel: (310) 540-4440.
ROCKLIN: Filati Yarns, 4810 Granite Dr., Suite A-7, Rocklin, CA 95677. Tel: (800) 398-9043.
SAN FRANCISCO: Greenwich Yarns, 2073 Greenwich Street, San Francisco, CA 94123. Tel: (415) 567-2535. Website: www.greenwichyarn.citysearch.com
SANTA BARBARA: In Stitches, 5 East Figueroa, Santa Barbara, CA 93101. Tel: (805) 962 9343. Website: www.institchesyarns.com
SANTA MONICA: L'Atelier on Montana, 1202 Montana Avenue, Santa Monica, CA 90403. Tel: (310) 394-4665.
Wild Fiber, 1453 E. 14th Street, Santa Monica, CA 90404. Tel: (310) 458 2748.
STUDIO CITY: La Knitterie Parisienne, 12642-44 Ventura Boulevard, Studio City, CA 91604. Tel: (818) 766-1515.
THOUSAND OAKS: Eva's Needleworks, 1321 East Thousand Oaks Boulevard, Thousand Oaks, CA 91360. Tel: (803) 379-0722.

COLORADO
COLORADO SPRINGS: Needleworks by Holly Berry, 2409 West Colorado Avenue, CO 80904. Tel: (719) 636-1002.
DENVER: Strawberry Tree, 2200 S Monaco Parkway, Denver, CO 80222. Tel: (303) 759-4244.
LAKEWOOD: Showers of Flowers, 6900 West Colfax Ave., Lakewood. Tel: (303) 233-2525. Website: www.showersofflowers.com
LONGMONT: Over the Moon, 600 S Airport Road, Bldg A, Ste D, Longmont, CO 80503. Tel: (303) 485-6778. Website: over-the-moon.com

CONNECTICUT
AVON: The Wool Connection, 34 East Main Street, Avon. Tel: (860) 678-1710.
DEEP RIVER: Yarns Down Under, 37C Hillside Terrace, Deep River, CT 06417. Tel: (860) 526-9986. Website: www.yarnsdownunder.com
MYSTIC: Mystic River Yarns, 14 Holmes Street, Mystic, CT 06355. Tel: (860) 536-4305.
SOUTHBURY: Selma's Yarn & Needleworks, 450 Heritage Road, Southbury. Tel: (203) 264-4838. Website: www.selmasyarns.com
WESTPORT: Hook 'N' Needle, 1869 Post Road East, Westport, CT 06880. Tel: (203) 259-5119. Website: www.hook-n-needle.com
WOODBRIDGE: The Yarn Barn, 24 Selden St., Woodbridge, CT 06525. Tel: (203) 389-5117. Website: www.theyarnbarn.com

GEORGIA
ATLANTA: Strings & Strands, 4632 Wieuca Road, Atlanta, GA 30342. Tel: (404) 252-9662.

ILLINOIS
CLARENDON HILLS: Flying Colors Inc., 15 Walker Avenue, Clarendon Hills, IL 60514. Tel: (630) 325-0888.
CHICAGO: Weaving Workshop, 2218 N Lincoln Avenue, Chicago, IL 60614. Tel: (773) 929-5776.

OAK PARK: Tangled Web Fibers, 177 S Oak Park Rd., Oak Park, IL 60302. Tel: (708) 445-8335. Website: www.tangledwebfibers.com
NORTHBROOK: Three Bags Full, 1856 Walters Ave., Northbrook, IL 60062. Tel: (847) 291-9933.
ST. CHARLES: The Fine Line Creative Arts Center, 6 N 158 Crane Road, St. Charles, IL 60175. Tel: (630) 584-9443.
SPRINGFIELD: Nancy's Knitworks, 1650 West Wabash Avenue, Springfield, IL 62704. Tel: (217) 546-0600.

INDIANA
FORT WAYNE: Cass Street Depot, 1044 Cass Street, Fort Wayne, IN 46802. Tel: (219) 420-2277. Website: www.cassstreetdepot.com
INDIANAPOLIS: Mass Avenue Knit Shop, 521 East North Street, Indianapolis, IN 46204. Tel: (800) 675-8565.

KANSAS
ANDOVER: Whimsies, 307 North Andover Rd., Andover, KS 67002. Tel: (316) 733-8881.
LAWRENCE: The Yarn Barn, 930 Mass Avenue, Lawrence, KS 66044. Tel: (800) 468-0035.

KENTUCKY
LOUISVILLE: Handknitters Limited, 11726 Main St., Louisville, KY 40243. Tel: (502) 254-9276. Website: www.handknittersltd.com

MAINE
CAMDEN: Stitchery Square, 11 Elm Street, Camden, ME 04843. Tel: (207) 236-9773. Website: www.stitching.com/stitcherysquare
FREEPORT: Grace Robinson & Co., 208 US Route 1, Suite 1, Freeport, ME 04032. Tel: (207) 865 6110.
HANCOCK: Shirley's Yarn & Crafts, Route 1, Hancock, ME 04640. Tel: (207) 667-7158.

MARYLAND
ANNAPOLIS: Yarn Garden, 2303 I Forest Dr., Annapolis, MD 21401. Tel: (410) 224-2033.
BALTIMORE: Woolworks, 6305 Falls Rd., Baltimore, MD 21209. Tel: (410) 337-9030.

BETHESDA: The Needlework Loft, 4706 Bethesda Avenue, Bethesda, MD. Tel: (301) 652-8688.
Yarns International, 5110 Ridgefield Rd., Bethesda, MD 20816. Tel: (301) 913-2980.
GLYNDON: Woolstock, 4848 Butler Road, Glyndon, MD 21071. Tel: (410) 517-1020.

MASSACHUSETTS
BROOKLINE VILLAGE: A Good Yarn, 4 Station Street, Brookline Village, MA 02447. Tel: (617) 731-4900. Website: www.agoodyarnonline.com
CAMBRIDGE: Woolcott & Co, 61 JFK Street, Cambridge, MA 02138-4931. Tel: (617) 547-2837.
DENNIS: Ladybug Knitting Shop, 612 Route 6, Dennis, MA 02638. Tel: (508) 385-2662. Website: www.ladybugknitting.com
DUXBURY: The Wool Basket, 19 Depot St., Duxbury, MA 02332. Tel: (781) 934-2700.
HARVARD: The Fiber Loft, 9 Massachusetts Ave., Harvard, MA 01451. Tel: (800) 874-9276.
LENOX: Colorful Stitches, 48 Main Street, Lenox, MA 01240. Tel: (800) 413-6111. Website: www.colorful-stitches.com
LEXINGTON: Wild & Woolly Studio, 7A Meriam Street, Lexington, MA 02173. Tel: (781) 861-7717.
MILTON: Snow Goose, 10 Bassett Street, Milton Market Place, Milton, MA 02186. Tel: (617) 698-1190.
NORTHAMPTON: Northampton Wools, 11 Pleasant Street, Northampton, MA 01060. Tel: (413) 586-4331.
WORCESTER: Knit Latte, 1062 Pleasant St., Worcester, MA 01602. Tel: (508) 754-6300.

MICHIGAN
BIRMINGHAM: Knitting Room, 251 Merrill, Birmingham, MI 48009. Tel: (248) 540-3623. Website: www.knittingroom.com
GRAND HAVEN: The Fibre House, 117

Washington Street, Grand Haven, MI 49417. Tel: (616) 844-2497. Website: www.forknitters.com
TRAVERSE CITY: Lost Art Yarn Shoppe, 123 East Front Street, Traverse City, MI 49684. Tel: (231) 941-1263.
WYOMING: Threadbender Yarn Shop, 2767 44th Street SW, Wyoming, MI 49509. Tel: (888) 531-6642.
YPSILANTE: Knit A Round Yarn Shop, 2888 Washtinaw Avenue, Ypsilante, MI 48197. Tel: (734) 528-5648.

MINNESOTA
MINNEAPOLIS: Linden Hills Yarn, 2720 W 43rd Street, Minneapolis, MN 55410. Tel: (612) 929-1255.
Needleworks Unlimited, 3006 W 50th Street, Minneapolis, MN 55410. Tel: (612) 925-2454.
MINNETONKA: Skeins, 11309 Highway 7, Minnetonka, MN 55305. Tel: (952) 939-4166.
ST. PAUL: The Yarnery KMK Crafts, 840 Grand Avenue, St. Paul, MN 55105. Tel: (651) 222-5793.
WHITE BEAR LAKE: A Sheepy Yarn Shoppe, 2185 Third Street, White Bear Lake, MN 55110. Tel: (800) 480-5462.

MONTANA
STEVENSVILLE: Wild West Wools, 3920 Suite B Highway 93N, Stevensville, MT 59870. Tel: (406) 777-4114.

NEBRASKA
OMAHA: Personal Threads Boutique, 8025 W Dodge Road, Omaha, NE 68114. Tel: (402) 391-7733. Website: www.personalthreads.com

NEW HAMPSHIRE
CONCORD: Elegant Ewe, 71 South Main St., Concord, NH 03301. Tel: (603) 226-0066.
EXETER: Charlotte's Web, Exeter Village Shops, 137 Epping Road, Route 27, Exeter, NH 03833. Tel: (888) 244-6460.

NASHUA: Rowan USA, 4 Townsend West, Nashua, NH. Tel: (603) 886-5041/5043.

NEW JERSEY

CHATHAM: Stitching Bee, 240A Main Street, Chatham, NJ 07928. Tel: (973) 635-6691. Website: www.thestitchingbee.com

HOBOKEN: Hoboken Handknits, 671 Willow Ave., Hoboken, NJ 07030. Tel: (201) 653-2545.

LAMBERTVILLE: Simply Knit, 23 Church Street, Lambertville, NJ 08530. Tel: (609) 397-7101.

PRINCETON: Glenmarle Woolworks, 301 North Harrison Street, Princeton, NJ 08540. Tel: (609) 921-3022.

NEW MEXICO

ALBUQUERQUE: Village Wools, 3801 San Mateo Avenue NE, Albuquerque, NM 87110. Tel: (505) 883-2919.

SANTA FE: Needle's Eye, 839 Paseo de Peralta, Santa Fe, NM 87501. Tel: (505) 982-0706.

NEW YORK

BEDFORD HILLS: Lee's Yarn Center, 733 N Bedford Road, Bedford Hills, NY 10507. Tel: (914) 244-3400. Website: www.leesyarn.com

BUFFALO: Elmwood Yarn Shop, 1639 Hertel Ave., Buffalo, NY 14216. Tel: (716) 834-7580.

GARDEN CITY: Garden City Stitches, 725 Franklin Avenue, Garden City, NY 11530. Tel: (516) 739-5648. Website: www.gardencitystitches.com

HUNTINGTON: Knitting Corner, 718 New York Avenue, Huntington, NY 11743. Tel: (631) 421-2660.

ITHACA: The Homespun Boutique, 314 East State St., Ithaca, NY 14850. Tel: (607) 277-0954.

MIDDLETOWN: Bonnie's Cozy Knits. Tel: (845) 344-0229.

NEW YORK CITY: Downtown Yarns, 45 Avenue A, New York, NY 10009. Tel: (212) 995-5991. Lion & The Lamb, 1460 Lexington Avenue, New York, NY 10128. Tel: (212) 876-4303. The Yarn Company, 2274 Broadway, New York,

NY 10024. Tel: (212) 787-7878. Yarn Connection, 218 Madison Ave., New York, NY 10016. Tel: (212) 684-5099. Woolgathering, 318 E 84th Street, New York, NY 10028. Tel: (212) 734-4747.

SKANEATELES: Elegant Needles, 7 Jordan St., Skaneateles, NY 13152. Tel: (315) 685-9276.

NORTH CAROLINA

GREENSBORO: Yarn Etc., 231 South Elm St., Greensboro, NC 27401. Tel: (336) 370-1233.

RALEIGH: Great Yarns, 1208 Ridge Road, Raleigh, NC. Tel: (919) 832-3599.

WILSON: Knit Wit, 1-B Ward Boulevard N, Wilson, NC 27893. Tel: (252) 291-8149.

NORTH DAKOTA

FARGO: Yarn Renaissance, 1226 S University Drive, Fargo, ND 58103. Tel: (701) 280-1478.

OHIO

AURORA: Edie's Knit Shop, 214 Chillicothe Road, Aurora, OH 44202. Tel: (330) 562-7226.

CINCINNATI: One More Stitch, 2030 Madison Rd., Cincinnati, OH 45208. Tel: (513) 533-1170. Wizard Weavers, 2701 Observatory Road, Cincinnati, OH 45208. Tel: (513) 871-5750.

CLEVELAND: Fine Points, 12620 Larchmere Boulevard, Cleveland, OH 44120. Tel: (216) 229-6644. Website: www.finepoints.com

COLUMBUS: Wolfe Fiber Art, 1188 West 5th Ave., Columbus, OH 43212. Tel: (614) 487-9980.

OREGON

ASHLAND: Web-sters, 11 North Main Street, Ashland, OR 97520. Tel: (800) 482-9801. Website: www.yarnatwebsters.com

COOS BAY: My Yarn Shop, 264 B Broadway, Coos Bay, OR 97420. Tel: (888) 664-9276. Website: www.myyarnshop.com

LAKE OSWEGO: Molehill Farm, 16722 SW Boones Ferry Road, Lake Oswego, OR 97035. Tel: (503) 697-9554.

PORTLAND: Northwest Wools, 3524 SW Troy Street, Portland, OR 97219. Tel: (503) 244-

5024. Website: www.northwestwools.com Yarn Garden, 1413 SE Hawthorne Boulevard, Portland, OR 97214. Tel: (503) 239-7950. Website: www.yarngarden.net

PENNSYLVANIA

KENNETT SQUARE: Wool Gathering, 131 East State St, Kennett Square, PA 19348. Tel: (610) 444-8236.

PHILADELPHIA: Sophie's Yarn, 2017 Locust Street, Philadelphia, PA 19103. Tel: (215) 977-9276.

Tangled Web. 7900 Germantown Avenue, Philadelphia, PA. Tel: (215) 242-1271.

SEWICKLEY: Yarns Unlimited, 435 Beaver St., Sewickley, PA 15143. Tel: (412) 741-8894.

RHODE ISLAND

PROVIDENCE: A Stitch Above Ltd., 190 Wayland Avenue, Providence, RI 02906. Tel: (800) 949-5648. Website: www.astitchaboveknitting.com

TIVERTON: Sakonnet Purls, 3988 Main Road, Tiverton, RI 02878. Tel: (888) 624-9902. Website: www.sakonnetpurls.com

SOUTH CAROLINA

AIKEN: Barbara Sue Brodie Needlepoint & Yarn, 148 Lauren Street, Aiken, SC 29801. Tel: (803) 644-0990.

TENNESSEE

NASHVILLE: Angel Hair Yarn Co., 4121 Hillsboro Park, #205, Nashville, TN 37215. Tel: (615) 269-8833. Website: www.angelhairyarn.com

TEXAS

SAN ANTONIO: The Yarn Barn of San Antonio, 4300 McCullough, San Antonio, TX 78212. Tel: (210) 826-3679.

VERMONT

WOODSTOCK: The Whippletree, 7 Central St., Woodstock, VT 05091. Tel: (802) 457-1325 .

VIRGINIA

CHARLOTTESVILLE: It's A Stitch Inc., 188 Zan

Road, Charlottesville, VA 22901. Tel: (804) 973-0331.

FALLS CHURCH: Aylin's Woolgatherer, 7245 Arlington Blvd #318, Falls Church, VA 22042. Tel: (703) 573-1900. Website: www.aylins-wool.com

RICHMOND: Got Yarn, 2520 Professional Road, Richmond, VA 23235. Tel: (888) 242-4474. Website: www.gotyarn.com

The Knitting Basket, 5812 Grove Ave., Richmond, VA 23226. Tel: (804) 282-2909.

WASHINGTON

BAINBRIDGE ISLAND: Churchmouse Yarns and Teas, 118 Madrone Lane, Bainbridge Island, WA 98110. Tel: (206) 780-2686.

BELLEVUE: Skeins! Ltd., 10635 NE 8th Street, Suite 104, Bellevue, WA 98004. Tel: (425) 452-1248. Website: www.skeinslimited.com

OLYMPIA: Canvas Works, 317 N Capitol, Olympia, WA 98501. Tel: (360) 352-4481.

POULSBO: Wild & Wooly, 19020 Front Street, Poulsbo, WA 98370. Tel: (800) 743-2100. Website: www.wildwooly.com

SEATTLE: The Weaving Works, 4717 Brooklyn Avenue, NE, Seattle, WA 98105. Tel: (888) 524-1221. Website: www.weavingworks.com

WISCONSIN

APPLETON: Jane's Knitting Hutch, 132 E Wisconsin Avenue, Appleton, WI 54911. Tel: (920) 954-9001.

DELEVAN: Studio S Fiber Arts, W8903 Country Hwy A, Delevan, WI 53115. Tel: (608) 883-2123.

ELM GROVE: The Yarn House, 940 Elm Grove Rd., Elm Grove, WI 53122. Tel: (262) 786-5660.

MADISON: The Knitting Tree Inc., 2614 Monroe Street, Madison, WI 53711. Tel: (608) 238-0121.

MILWAUKEE: Ruhama's, 420 E Silver Spring Dr., Milwaukee, WI 53217. Tel: (414) 332-2660.

ROWAN STOCKISTS CANADA

DISTRIBUTOR: Diamond Yarn (Distributor), 9697 St. Laurent, Montreal, Quebec. Tel: (514) 388-6188.

ALBERTA

CALGARY: Birch Hill Yarns, 417-12445 Lake Fraser Drive SE, Calgary. Tel: (403) 271-4042.
Gina Brown's, 17, 6624 Centre Sr SE, Calgary. Tel: (403) 255-2200.

EDMONTON: Knit & Purl, 10412-124 Street, Edmonton. Tel: (403) 482 2150.
Wool Revival, 6513-112 Avenue, Edmonton. Tel: (403) 471-2749.

ST. ALBERT: Burwood House, 205 Carnegie Drive, St. Albert. Tel: (403) 459-4828.

BRITISH COLUMBIA

COQUITLAM: Village Crafts, 1936 Como Lake Avenue, Coquitlam. Tel: (604) 931- 6533.

DUNCAN: The Loom, Whippletree Junction, Box H, Duncan. Tel: (250) 746-5250.

PORT ALBERNI: Heartspun, 5242 Mary Street, Port Alberni. Tel: (250) 724-2285.

RICHMOND: Wool & Wicker, 120-12051 2nd Avenue, Richmond. Tel: (604) 275-1239.

VICTORIA: Beehave Wool Shop, 2207 Oak Bay Avenue, Victoria. Tel: (250) 598-2272.

WEST VANCOUVER: The Knit & Stitch Shoppe, 2460a Marine Drive, West Vancouver. Tel: (604) 922-1023.

MANITOBA

WINNIPEG: Ram Wools, 1266 Fife Street, Winnipeg. Tel: (204) 949-6868. Website: www.gaspard.ca/ramwools.htm

NOVA SCOTIA

BAADECK: Baadeck Yarns, 16 Chebucto Street, Baadeck. Tel: (902) 295-2993.

ONTARIO

ANCASTER: The Needle Emporium, 420 Wilson St. East, Ancaster. Tel: (800) 667-9167.

AURORA: Knit or Knot, 14800 Yong Street (Aurora Shopping Centre), Aurora.

Tel: (905) 713-1818.
Needles & Knits, 15040 Yonge Street, Aurora. Tel: (905) 713-2066.

CARLETON: Real Wool Shop, 142 Franktown Road, Carleton. Tel: (613) 257-2714.

LONDON: Christina Tandberg, Covent Garden Market, London. Tel: (800) 668-7903.

MYRTLE STATION: Ferguso's Knitting, 9585 Baldwin Street (Hwy 12), Ashburn.

OAKVILLE: The Wool Bin, 236 Lakeshore Road East, Oakville. Tel: (905) 845-9512.

OTTAWA: Wool Tyme, #2 - 190 Colonnade Road S, Ottawa. Tel: 1-(888) 241-7653. Website: www.wool-tyme.com
Yarn Forward, 581 Bank Street, Ottawa. Tel: (877) yar-nfwd.
Your Creation, 3767 Mapleshore Drive, Kemptville, Ottawa. Tel: (613) 826 3261.

TORONTO: Passionknit Ltd., 3467 Yonge Street, Toronto. Tel: (416) 322-0688.
Romni Wools Ltd., 658 Queen Street West, Toronto. Tel: (416) 703-0202.
Village Yarns, 4895 Dundas Street West, Toronto. Tel: (416) 232-2361.
The Wool Mill, 2170 Danorth Avenue, Toronto. Tel: (416) 696-2670.
The Yarn Boutique, 1719A Bloor West, Toronto. Tel: (416) 760-9129.

STRATFORD: D&S Craft Supplies, 165 Downie Street, Stratford. Tel: (519) 273-7962.

QUEBEC

MONTREAL: A la Tricoteuse, 779 Rachel Est, Montreal. Tel: (514) 527-2451.

ST. LAMBERT: Saute Mouton, 20 Webster, St. Lambert. Tel: (514) 671-1155.

QUEBEC CITY: La Dauphine, 1487 Chemin Ste-Foy, Quebec City. Tel: (418) 527-3030.

SASKATCHEWAN

SASKATOON: Prairie Lily Knitting & Weaving Shop, 7-1730 Quebec Avenue, Saskatoon. Tel: (306) 665-2771.

index

acknowledgments

I would like to thank Susan Berry for sharing the vision, John Heseltine for his discerning eye, Anne Wilson for her elegant design, Sally Harding for her professionalism, Sally Lee for her perfectionism, enthusiasm, and tireless hard work (well, everything), Hannah Davis for her wisdom and generosity of spirit, and Julia Bird for her inherent style. I would also like to thank Quadrille for "seeing it": in particular Jane O'Shea, for her unfailing encouragement and support, and Mary Evans and Helen Lewis for offering a guiding hand. I am grateful, too, to Stephen Sheard of Coats plc (Rowan and Jaeger yarns) for his enthusiastic and continued support, and to Ann Hinchcliffe for her patience and efficiency. Above all, I would like to thank my loving, long-suffering family and friends for their support, and the suppers! You all made it happen, thank you!